19

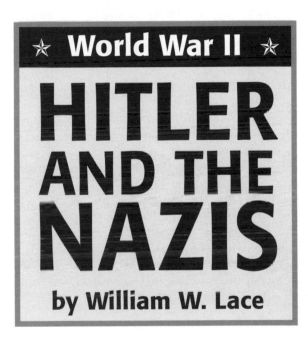

★ World War II ★

HITLER AND THE NAZIS

by William W. Lace

Lucent Books, P.O. Box 289011, San Diego, CA 92198-9011

Titles in The American War Library series include:

World War II
Hitler and the Nazis
Kamikazes
Leaders and Generals
Life as a POW
Life of an American Soldier in
  Europe
Strategic Battles in Europe
Strategic Battles in the Pacific
The War at Home
Weapons of War

The Civil War
Leaders of the North and South
Life Among the Soldiers and
  Cavalry
Lincoln and the Abolition of
  Slavery
Strategic Battles
Weapons of War

Library of Congress Cataloging-in-Publication Data

Lace, William W.
    Hitler and the Nazis / by William W. Lace
        p.   cm.—(The American war library series)
    Includes bibliographical references (p.)and index.
    Summary: Discusses Adolf Hitler, his rise to power, the
Nazification of Germany, the fate of the Jews, and the Third
Reich during World War II.
    ISBN 1-56006-372-6 (lib. alk. paper)
    1. Hitler, Adolf, 1889–1945 Juvenile literature. 2. Germany—
Politics and government—1933–1945 Juvenile literature.
3. National socialism Juvenile literature. 4. Holocaust, Jewish
(1939–1945) Juvenile literature. [1. Hitler, Adolf, 1889–1945.
2. National socialism. 3. Holocaust, Jewish (1939–1945)
4. Germany—Politics and government—1933–1945.] I. Title
II. Series.
DD247.H5L243   2000
943.086'092—dc21   99-24600
[B]   CIP

★ Contents ★

A Nation Forged by War

The United States, like many nations, was forged and defined by war. Despite Benjamin Franklin's opinion that "There never was a good war or a bad peace," the United States owes its very existence to the War of Independence, one to which Franklin wholeheartedly subscribed. The country forged by war in 1776 was tempered and made stronger by the Civil War in the 1860s.

The Texas Revolution, the Mexican-American War, and the Spanish-American War expanded the country's borders and gave it overseas possessions. These wars made the United States a world power, but this status came with a price, as the nation became a key but reluctant player in both World War I and World War II.

Each successive war further defined the country's role on the world stage. Following World War II, U.S. foreign policy redefined itself to focus on the role of defender, not only of the freedom of its own citizens, but also of the freedom of people everywhere. During the cold war that followed World War II until the collapse of the Soviet Union, defending the world meant fighting communism. This goal, manifested in the Korean and Vietnam conflicts, proved elusive, and soured the American public on its achievability. As the United States emerged as the world's sole superpower, American foreign policy has been guided less by national interest and more on protecting international human rights. But as involvement in Somalia and Kosovo prove, this goal has been equally elusive.

As a result, the country's view of itself changed. Bolstered by victories in World Wars I and II, Americans first relished the role of protector. But, as war followed war in a seemingly endless procession, Americans began to doubt their leaders, their motives, and themselves. The Vietnam War especially caused people to question the validity of sending its young people to die in places where they were not particularly wanted and for people who did not seem especially grateful.

While the most obvious changes brought about by America's wars have been geopolitical in nature, many other aspects of society have been touched. War often does not bring about change directly, but acts instead like the catalyst in a chemical reaction, accelerating changes already in progress.

Some of these changes have been societal. The role of women in the United States had been slowly changing, but World War II put thousands into the workforce and into uniform. They might have gone back to being housewives after the war, but equality, once experienced, would not be forgotten.

Likewise, wars have accelerated technological change. The necessity for faster airplanes and a more destructive bomb led to the development of jet planes and nuclear energy. Artificial fibers developed for parachutes in the 1940s were used in the clothing of the 1950s.

Lucent Books' American War Library covers key wars in the development of the nation. Each war is covered in several volumes, to allow for more detail, context, and to provide volumes on often neglected subjects, such as the kamikazes of World War II, or weapons used in the Civil War. As with all Lucent Books, notes, annotated bibliographies, and appendixes such as glossaries give students a launching point for further research. In addition, sidebars and archival photographs enhance the text. Together, each volume in The American War Library will aid students in understanding how America's wars have shaped and changed its politics, economics, and society.

Devils Incarnate?

The term "Nazi" immediately calls forth a host of mental pictures, each one more grim and unrelenting. Ranks of torch-carrying men tramp through the streets, red-black-white swastika armbands standing out on the sleeves of their brown shirts. Waves of bombers pound a city into rubble while columns of tanks crush all opposition. A corpse, starved to little more than a skeleton, is tossed into a pit with hundreds of others.

The sharpest picture of all is of a single man, Adolf Hitler—a lock of hair falling over his forehead, an almost comically short mustache on his lip—screaming into a microphone. He pauses, hands on hips. He glares defiantly as the huge crowd cheers, right arms extended out in stiff salute.

"Nazi" has gone far beyond its original meaning, a shortened version of *Nationalsozialistische Deutsche Arbeiterpartei*, National Socialist German Workers Party. It has become synonymous with brutality, cruelty, racism, and genocide. Accordingly, anyone who was a Nazi is assumed to have been an embodiment of evil.

Indeed, barbarism existed in Nazi Germany on a scale unmatched in European

Gesturing wildly, Adolf Hitler gives a speech at a rally in Nuremberg, Germany.

history. The horrors of World War II, inflicted both on the battlefield and to innocent civilians, must be laid at the feet of Hitler and his party cronies. And yet, not all the Nazis were heartless butchers and not all the butchery was done by Nazis. Yes, the storm troopers and the members of the feared state police, the *Gestapo*, were Nazis, but so might have been the local postman, the shopkeeper, the schoolteacher, or even the minister.

Power Brings Changes

The Nazis, as most political movements do, underwent changes as their power increased. The Nazis of the early 1920s were not like those of the late 1930s, when the party was firmly entrenched and thousands joined because it was the practical and profitable thing to do.

Even in the early days, however, people joined the Nazi Party for different reasons. Some were embittered by Germany's defeat in World War I. Some hated the Communists. Some hated the Jews. Some loved nothing more than a good street brawl. It was always part of Hitler's genius that he was able to weld diverse elements into a unit, telling all listeners what they wanted to hear.

Weld them he did, and in the space of two decades Hitler turned a tiny band of misfits and malcontents into a military power that challenged the rest of the world. The challenge was answered, and the result was World War II.

Kneeling above a mass grave, a civilian of a country overrun by the Nazis is about to be executed by a member of an SS Action Group.

The war was a tragic chapter in the annals of humanity, and all the more tragic because it probably could have been prevented. It was not prevented because people did not take Hitler and the Nazis seriously—not local authorities, not the German government, not the rest of the world—until it was too late. Everyone underestimated Hitler, and the cost was 55 million lives.

Chapter 1

The Young Hitler

It is impossible to separate the Nazi Party from Adolf Hitler. He breathed life into it in 1919, and it largely died with him in 1945. He created the party's beliefs, its structure, even the outward symbols like the swastika. Its leaders swore allegiance, not to a constitution or a nation, but to the person of Hitler. He, not his party, led Germany down the path to war and destruction. Any study of the Nazis, therefore, must begin with a study of Hitler.

The man who later plunged Germany into a bloody war was not even a German but an Austrian, born on April 20, 1889, in the border village of Braunau am Inn. His mother, Klara Pölzl, pampered her son and smothered him with affection. His father, Alois Hitler, twenty-three years older than his wife, was a bitter man, as distant with Adolf as his wife was attentive.

Father and son argued constantly. Adolf later wrote in his political biography *Mein Kampf* (My Struggle) that his father wanted him to become a government official while he was determined to be an artist. The real reason probably was

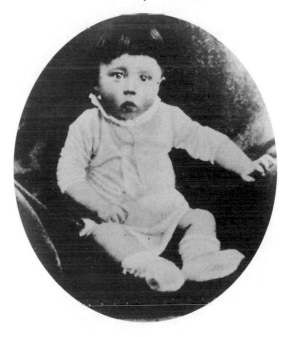

Adolf Hitler as a young child. The future dictator was born in Austria on April 20, 1889.

Adolf's poor performance in school in the town of Linz, where his family had moved in 1895. He seldom studied and quickly grew bored with subjects that did not interest him. He excelled in drawing and gymnastics but failed or barely passed everything else.

Hitler's problem was not that he lacked intelligence but rather, as one of his teachers, Dr. Eduard Hümer, wrote, that he "lacked self-discipline, being notoriously cantankerous, willful, arrogant, and bad-tempered. He had obvious difficulty in fitting in at school."[1]

Hitler had few friends among his schoolmates, doubtless because he thought himself far superior to them. Hümer wrote that "he demanded of his fellow pupils their unqualified subservience, fancying himself in the role of a leader."[2]

Blaming Others

As he would do for the rest of his life, Hitler blamed his failures on others, especially his teachers, whom he called "absolute tyrants."[3] He accused his teachers of failing to recognize his genius and originality. His experiences in school left Hitler with a deep resentment of both authority and anything intellectual. Later in his career, he constantly attempted to prove his superiority to others in fields where he had little or no experience. Germany lost World War II largely because Hitler constantly overruled his generals.

One of Hitler's teachers, Dr. Leopold Poetsch, made an impression on him that would be both lasting and fateful. Dr. Poetsch, a historian, was an outspoken German nationalist who thought all people of Germanic origin should combine into a single nation that would be the most powerful in Europe, if not the world. Hitler was transfixed. In *Mein Kampf,* he wrote,

There we [Hitler and his classmates] sat, often aflame with enthusiasm, sometimes even moved to tears. . . . He used our budding national fanaticism as a means of educating us, frequently appealing to our sense of national honor. . . . Though he had no such intention, it was then that I became a young revolutionary.[4]

Hitler's father died in 1903 at the age of sixty-four. Two years later, in the absence of any parental pressure to remain in school, Hitler left without graduating. School, he thought, was for ordinary people. He was special. He would be an artist.

For the next two years, Hitler did not attempt to become much of anything. He lived with his mother, allowing his father's small pension to support both of them. When other relatives urged him to get a job, he refused. Hitler later called these years "the hollowness of the life of leisure,"[5] but he was hardly idle. His one good friend, August Kubizek, wrote,

In reality, this chapter of his life was filled with unceasing activity. He sketched, he painted, he wrote poems

Hitler's parents, Alois (top) and Klara Hitler. Alois was a bitter, distant father, but Klara smothered young Adolf with affection.

and he read. I cannot remember that Adolf was ever idle or felt bored even for a single hour. . . . To be sure, he was as yet not very systematic. There was no apparent purpose, no clear goal. He only accumulated with unbounded energy impressions, experience and material. What would ever become of it all

remained an open question. He did nothing but search. He searched everywhere and always.[6]

The Dreamer

Hitler was full of dreams and only reluctantly let reality interrupt his dreaming. He had grand plans for rebuilding Linz. He strolled through the streets with paper and pencil, sketching his visions of opera houses, museums, churches, bridges. He planned a grand villa where he and Kubizek would live. With them would be Stefanie, a beautiful girl whom Hitler loved.

Stefanie was real enough, but their relationship was only imagined. She was two years older than Hitler and the daughter of a widow in Linz. As was typical, Hitler did not want to risk the reality of rejection. He never even spoke to Stefanie, preferring only to watch her as she walked through the town with her mother.

When Kubizek asked Hitler how he planned to pay for his grandiose plans, Hitler bought a lottery ticket. Even though he knew the tremendous odds against winning the top prize, he became convinced it would be his, and even drew up a household budget for his villa. When he failed to win he flew into a rage, blaming the government. Kubizek wrote, "Never did it occur to Adolf to reproach himself for having taken it for granted that the first prize belonged to him by right."[7]

Hitler refused to let his dreams die. He was convinced that he was destined for greatness. One night he and Kubizek saw a performance of the opera *Rienzi*, in which the hero rises from obscurity to become a tribune of Rome. Afterward, Hitler led Kubizek to the top of a hill outside Linz and there began to talk about his future. Kubizek wrote,

> It was a state of complete ecstasy and rapture, in which he transferred the character of *Rienzi* . . . with visionary power to the plane of his own ambitions. . . . Like flood waters breaking their dykes, his words burst forth from him. He conjured up in grandiose, inspiring pictures his own future and that of his people. . . . It was an unknown youth who spoke to me in that strange hour. He spoke of a special mission which one day would be entrusted to him. . . . Many years had to pass before I realized the significance of this enraptured hour for my friend.[8]

The Move to Vienna

Linz was too small a stage on which to play this new role. In the fall of 1907, the eighteen-year-old Hitler talked his mother into giving him part of his inheritance so that he could live in Vienna, the Austrian capital, and pursue a career as an artist. He left his mother behind, even though she was already ill with the breast cancer that would take her life later that year.

In October, Hitler took the entrance examination for the Academy of Art. He was rejected, but he vowed to stay in Vienna, improve his drawing technique, and

try for the Academy once more. He convinced Kubizek to join him, and the friends shared a small apartment. While Kubizek studied music, Hitler led a busy but aimless life. He read, drew, and even tried writing a play. He had received his inheritance from his mother and spent it on operas, sightseeing, books, and in coffeehouses. It should have been a carefree life but was not. Kubizek thought that Hitler "had become unbalanced. He would fly into temper at the slightest thing. . . . He was at odds with the world. Wherever he looked, he saw injustice, hate and enmity. Nothing was free from his criticism."[9]

In 1908, Kubizek went home to Linz for the summer. When he returned in November, Hitler had vanished, not even leaving an address. He had tried once more to enter the Academy of Art. This time the drawings that he had submitted were so poor that he was not even permitted to take the exam. He then tried to study architecture but found that he could not do so without a high school diploma.

Reality had finally caused Adolf Hitler's dreamworld to crumble. He was nineteen years old, had no career and no hope of one. He had spent practically all his inheritance. He was at last face-to-face with the realization that he was a failure. He could not bear to face Kubizek or return to Linz. Instead, he remained in Vienna, gradually sliding into abject poverty.

He had moved from the apartment he shared with Kubizek into a furnished room. When his money ran out in the summer of 1909, he was without a home. As long as the warm weather lasted, he slept on park benches or in doorways. When autumn came, however, he was forced to go to a shelter for homeless men. One of them who knew Hitler at the time, Reinhold Hanisch, said,

> On the very first day there sat next to the bed that had been allotted to me a man who had nothing on except an old torn pair of trousers—Hitler. His clothes were being cleaned of lice, since for days he had been wandering about without a roof and in a terribly neglected condition.[10]

Living with Hunger

Hitler had a tiny pension as an orphan, but it was not enough even to buy food. He swallowed his pride and managed to earn a little money shoveling snow, beating

---

The Piercing Eyes

Of the millions of Germans who came under the spell of Adolf Hitler's voice, only a few ever came close enough to him to encounter another physical attribute equally compelling—his eyes. In his book *The Young Hitler I Knew,* August Kubizek describes how, even as a boy, Hitler could almost hypnotize others with his gaze:

> The eyes were so outstanding that one didn't notice anything else. Never in my life have I seen any other person whose appearance—how shall I put it—was so completely dominated by the eyes. They were the light eyes of his mother, but her somewhat staring, penetrating gaze was even more marked in the son and had even more force and expressiveness. It was uncanny how those eyes could change their expression, especially when Adolf was speaking. To me his sonorous voice meant much less than the expression of his eyes. In fact, Adolf spoke with his eyes, and even when his lips were silent one knew what he wanted to say. When he first came to our house and I introduced him to my mother, she said to me in the evening, "What eyes your friend has!" And I remember quite distinctly that there was more fear than admiration in her words. If I am asked where

one could perceive, in his youth, this man's exceptional qualities, I can only answer, "In the eyes."

With their hypnotic gaze, Hitler's eyes were as compelling as his voice.

---

carpets, or carrying suitcases for travelers disembarking at Vienna's train station. With part of the money he earned, he bought pens, inks, and paper on which he painted postcards showing various views of the city. Still, there was never enough food. "Hunger was then my faithful bodyguard," he wrote in *Mein Kampf.* "He never left me for a moment and partook of all I had. . . . My life was a continual struggle with this pitiless friend."[11]

The four years (1909–1913) that Hitler spent as a vagrant in Vienna in his early twenties hardened him and also shaped his political philosophy. He might have been expected to turn toward communism, which was beginning to gain in strength throughout Europe, but communism was an international movement calling for universal brotherhood of the working classes. Hitler was far too much of a German nationalist to embrace such a philosophy. He never identified with the common people, but instead with those able to bend the masses to their will. Any movement that placed power with the people he dismissed as a "pestilential whore covered with the mask of social virtue and brotherly love."[12]

Just as important as Hitler's political views were his attitudes on race. Up to this point, Hitler's rage had been directed against everyone. He hated his teachers. He hated those at the Academy who had rejected him. He hated the wealthy people he saw in the streets, and he despised the poor with whom he had been thrown together. A German in spirit if not by birth,

he was disgusted by the mix he found in Vienna—Bohemians, Slavs, Serbs, Turks, and, above all, Jews, who made up 10 percent of the city's population.

In *Mein Kampf,* Hitler wrote that it was in Vienna that he first became truly aware of Jews. He wrote that

One day . . . I suddenly encountered an apparition in a black caftan [full-length overcoat] and black sidelocks [of hair]. Is this a Jew? was my first thought. For, to be sure, they had not looked like that in Linz. I observed the man furtively and curiously, but the longer I stared at this foreign face, scrutinizing feature for feature, the more my first question assumed a new form: Is this a German?[13]

An Earlier View

Kubizek, on the other hand, claimed that Hitler was firmly anti-Semitic before he ever went to Vienna. He described how many of the teachers at the school in Linz preached hatred of the Jews. He described a time when he and Hitler were walking past the small synagogue in Linz. "This shouldn't be here,"[14] Hitler muttered.

Hitler began to read the violently anti-Semitic literature widespread in Vienna. He began to see the Jews as the focal point of all his hatreds. The Jews, he claimed, were at the heart of the ruling Social Democratic Party that exploited the people. The Jews were responsible for poverty, pornography, prostitution, crime. In short,

Hitler's Jewish Question

The man who made anti-Semitism the cornerstone of his philosophy and who caused the deaths of millions of Jews, may himself have been part Jewish. When rumors about Hitler's background began to circulate in 1930, he instructed a Nazi lawyer, Hans Frank, who eventually was governor-general of conquered Poland and was hanged as a war criminal, to investigate. As quoted in Joachim Fest's *The Face of the Third Reich,* Frank's confidential report to Hitler read, in part:

> Hitler's father was the illegitimate child of a cook named [Maria Anna] Schickelgruber, from Leonding, near Linz, employed in a household at Graz. This cook Schickelgruber, the grandmother of Adolf Hitler, was working for a Jewish family named Frankenberger when she gave birth to her child. [Actually, Maria Schickelgruber became pregnant while working for the Frankenbergers and gave birth to the baby after she left their employment.] At that time—this happened in the 1830s—Frankenberger paid Schickelgruber on be-

half of his son, then about nineteen, a paternity allowance from the time of her child's birth up to his fourteenth year. There was also a correspondence between these Frankenbergers and Hitler's grandmother, the general trend of which was the unexpressed common knowledge of the correspondents that Schickelgruber's child had been conceived in circumstances which rendered the Frankenbergers liable to pay a paternity allowance.

> Five years after the son, Alois, was born, Maria Schickelgruber married Johann Heidler. Only when he was forty did Alois Schickelgruber have his name changed to that of his stepfather. The name was changed in the birth register but was misspelled as "Hitler."

> Hitler's feelings about his father's family were to be made clear shortly after Germany annexed Austria in 1938. The village of Döllersheim, the site of the church in which the births were recorded and where his father and grandmother were buried, was turned into an army training base. No trace of the graves remains.

the Jews were to blame for everything that plagued modern society. He wrote,

> Was there any form of filth or profligacy [extravagant self-indulgence], particularly in cultural life, without at least one Jew involved in it? If you cut even cautiously into such an abscess, you found, like a maggot in a rotting body, often dazzled by the sudden light—a [little Jew]![15]

Hitler was intelligent but not an intellectual. He was unable to see the complex-

ities of social problems and instead preferred to lock onto a single, tangible root cause—in his case, the Jews. His hatred of the Jews was not merely a result of his racism but rather of his deeply disturbed personality. All his life, he seemed to have been thwarted by outside forces. In Vienna, those phantom forces took human shape.

In addition to political philosophy, Hitler learned political techniques in Vienna. He saw how the Social Democratic Party consolidated its power. He attended rallies and listened to speeches.

Through Hitler, the Social Democrats' tactics of 1910 would be turned into the Nazi tactics of the 1930s. In *Mein Kampf* he wrote,

> I understood the infamous spiritual terror which this movement [Social Democrats] exerts. . . . At a given sign it unleashes a veritable barrage of lies and slanders against whatever adversary seems most dangerous. . . . This is a tactic based on precise calculation of all human weakness, and its result will lead to success with almost mathematical certainty. . . .
>
> I achieved an equal understanding of the importance of physical terror toward the individual and the masses. . . . For while in the ranks of their supporters the victory achieved seems a triumph of the justice of their own cause, the defeated adversary in most cases despairs of the success of any further resistance.[16]

In Munich

Hitler left Vienna in May 1913. He wrote that he could no longer stand living amid "this conglomerate spectacle of heterogeneous races,"[17] but the real reason was probably to avoid serving in the Austrian army. He had been ordered up for military duty every year since 1910 but had failed to report. Now, with the police seeking him, he moved across the German border to Munich.

In Munich, he lived with a tailor and his family. Although he later described the time as "by far the happiest time of my life,"[18] he lived much the same way he had in Vienna, selling a few drawings and barely earning enough money to rent his room and buy food. When he was finally found by the Austrian police, he lied, claiming he had not fled to escape military service. He agreed to report for examination at Salzburg, where in February 1914 he was rejected as physically unfit.

When Archduke Ferdinand of Austria was assassinated in June, touching off the conflict that became World War I, Hitler was ecstatic. He now had a purpose in life. "I believed that it was not a case of Austria fighting to get satisfaction from Serbia, but rather a case of Germany fighting for her own existence,"[19] he wrote. When war was declared, he joined a cheering crowd in Munich's Odeonplatz. A photograph of the event shows him, shouting with the rest, his eyes shining with excitement.

Although an Austrian, he volunteered for the German army and was accepted. Ten weeks later he was on the battle lines in France. Many of Hitler's later stories about his early life stretch the truth, but there is no doubt of the excellence of his war record. He was wounded twice and received two medals, one of which, the Iron Cross First Class, was seldom given to any but officers. He proudly wore it the rest of his life.

Even though his bravery was unquestioned, he was not popular with his com-

Hitler made this sketch of an inn while living in Munich. By selling his drawings, he barely earned enough money for food and rent.

rades. He kept to himself and made no effort to fit in with them. He bored his fellow soldiers with long-winded political speeches. One member of his regiment wrote that Hitler was

a peculiar fellow. He sat in the corner of our mess [dining hall] holding his head between his hands, in deep contemplation. Suddenly he would leap up, and, running about excitedly, say that in spite of our big guns, victory would be denied us, for the invisible foes of the German people [the Jews] were a greater danger than the biggest cannon of the enemy.[20]

Swearing Revenge

Just a month before the war ended in November 1918, Hitler was caught in a gas attack that almost blinded him. He was recovering in a hospital near Berlin when an army chaplain told him that Germany had

Hitler (front row, far left) poses with his unit during World War I. He was not liked by his fellow soldiers, who found Hitler to be an isolated and peculiar man.

signed an armistice with the victorious Allies. He was overcome with both grief and anger. Germany had not been defeated, he swore. She had been betrayed—by the generals, by the politicians, by the Jews. He vowed to get revenge on Germany's enemies. He vowed to go into politics.

After the war, Hitler remained in the army. A republic had replaced the German monarchy, and all sorts of political parties fought for power. The military distrusted democracy and feared a Communist takeover, as had happened in Russia. Hitler, whose impassioned harangues against Communists and Jews had drawn the approval of his officers, was assigned to

investigate some of the political groups springing up in the southern German state of Bavaria to see if they posed any threat from the Left.

In September 1919 Hitler received orders to attend a meeting of the *Deutsche Arbeiterpartei* (DAP), or German Workers Party. Despite its grand name, the DAP claimed only a few dozen members. Hitler attended a meeting at which a speaker called for the unification of Austria and

Germany. Hitler jumped to his feet and rejected the notion of Germany joining with the non-Germanic parts of Austria. Instead, he shouted, all Germans everywhere should join in a single nation.

The next day, he received an invitation to join the DAP. At first, he wanted to decline. He wanted to found his own party, not join one, and certainly not one as disorganized as he perceived the DAP to be. Still, he was attracted to the group. He later wrote,

> After two days of agonized pondering and reflection, I finally came to the conviction that I had to take this step.

It was the most decisive resolve of my life. From here there was and could be no turning back.[21]

Adolf Hitler—the outsider, the misfit, the former vagrant—became DAP member number 555, a number which sounded impressive unless you knew that the party's numbering system started with 500. But this small group of malcontents—soon to be known as the Nazis—had found its leader, the man who would take them to ultimate power and their country to ultimate destruction.

Chapter 2

The Road to Power

In 1919, the German Workers Party (DAP) had few members, a muddled political philosophy, little money, and no influence. It did, however, have Adolf Hitler—enough to propel it in only fifteen years to becoming the ruling party in Germany.

The end of World War I left Germany in chaos. Unemployment was high; inflation was so rampant that people used currency as wallpaper. There was a democratic government, but Germany had no tradition of democracy. The Weimar Republic, named for the city in which the constitution was drafted, was despised and distrusted by both the Left and Right. More than forty political parties jockeyed for power. Communists and workers' groups fought street battles against the right-wing *Freikorps*, or Free Corps, hired troops made up mostly of former soldiers.

Most Germans feared a Communist takeover, greatly increasing the appeal of right-wing groups such as the DAP. The party had been created on January 2, 1919, by the combination of two such groups. Although its name implied a workers' party,

German currency was almost worthless after World War I. Here a man uses paper money to cover a wall.

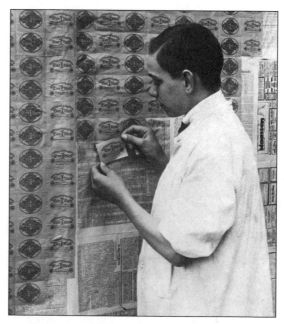

the DAP was made up mostly of men from the middle and lower middle classes. They were mostly between twenty-five and thirty. Many were former soldiers, violent men now left without a profession. They were united by a fierce German nationalism, a hatred of the Jews, a distrust of democracy, and a fear of communism.

During its first few months, the DAP did little besides talk and debate. That changed soon after Hitler joined the party. He organized a public rally in February 1920, renting a hall in Munich that would hold nearly two thousand people. His fellow party members were doubtful, but the hall was almost filled by those curious about the new group.

The Munichers loved entertainment, and Hitler did not disappoint them. He ranted for nearly four hours, blaming Germany's defeat on the Jews and on the politicians he called the "November criminals," the armistice having been signed in November 1918. He outlined the twenty-five points of the DAP platform. All Germanic people would be united in one nation, which would be entitled by virtue of its superior blood to take *Lebensraum*, or living space, from less worthy groups. Only those of pure "Aryan" blood, the Aryans supposedly having been the ancient ancestors of the Germans, could be citizens. Other people would serve the German master race. The Jews, as defilers of pure German blood, would have no place at all. Hitler would later view the speech as the turning point, where the party, "burst the narrow bonds of a small club and for the first time exerted a determining influence on the mightiest factor of our time: public opinion."[22]

Socialism Rejected

A week later, the DAP officially changed its name to the *Nationalsozialistische Deutsche Arbeiterpartei*—the National Socialist German Workers Party—called "Nazi" for short. The "socialist" part of the name was chosen to convey that this was a party of workers, but one exclusively German in character. In fact, Hitler did not view the Nazis as a political party in the traditional sense. He disdained democratic political processes and thought rather in terms of a mass movement that would, in time, topple the republic.

Hitler knew, however, that it would take far more than words to bring the masses to the Nazi cause. Words were fine for intellectuals, but the masses needed visible symbols to rally behind. "Whoever wishes to win over the masses must know the key that will open the door to their hearts," he wrote. "It is not objectivity . . . but a determined will, backed up by power where necessary."[23]

Hitler adopted as the Nazis' primary symbol the swastika—*Hakenkreuz* (crooked cross) in German. The swastika had been used in various societies for thousands of years, most lately by the *Freikorps* and other right-wing groups. Hitler's only change was to make the arms of the swastika point clockwise instead of counterclockwise.

Hitler also chose—after searching through library books—the version of the eagle that would go atop Nazi banners. The banners, soon to be a staple of Nazi rallies and parades, featured the eagle perched atop a swastika. Under the swastika was the local party shield with the motto *Deutschland, Erwacht!*—"Germany, Awaken!"

By 1920, the greeting of *Heil*, which could be translated as "saved" or "healed," had come into use, along with the right arm held out stiffly at an angle as a salute. Later, when Hitler was the supreme leader of the party, the greeting was changed to "*Heil*, Hitler."

While written words might not stir the hearts of the people, spoken words could be powerful indeed. Hitler knew from his experiences as an education officer in the army that he was an effective speaker. His secret was that he was always in tune with his audience. A fellow Nazi, Otto Strasser, later wrote,

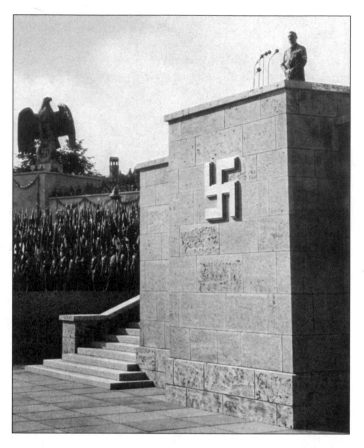

Accompanied by the emblems he chose to symbolize the Nazi party—the swastika and the eagle—Hitler speaks at one of the rallies held at Nuremberg during the 1930s.

Hitler responds to the vibration of the human heart with the delicacy of a seismograph, or perhaps of a wireless receiving set, enabling him, with a certainty with which no conscious gift could endow him, to act as a loudspeaker proclaiming the most secret desires, the least admissible instincts, the sufferings, and personal revolts of a whole nation. . . . Adolf Hitler enters a hall. He sniffs the air. For a minute he gropes, feels his way, senses the atmosphere. Suddenly he bursts forth. His words go like an arrow to their target, he touches each private wound on the raw, liberating the mass unconscious, expressing its innermost aspirations, telling it what it most wants to hear.[24]

Birth of the SA

Other groups had effective speakers too, and the practice of the time was to have gangs of thugs to protect one's own rallies or to disrupt the rallies of rivals. Hitler organized his own strong-arm band in the summer of 1920, which was formally established the next year as the *Sturmabteilung* (Storm Detachment). The members of the SA, as it came to be known, were called storm troopers or "brownshirts" from the uniforms they wore. By the fall of 1922 there were more than fifteen thousand men in the SA.

Indeed, the SA grew so large and powerful that Hitler saw it as an eventual threat. He needed a smaller force loyal only to him. In 1923 he organized the *Stabswache* (Headquarters Guard), later to become the *Schutzstaffel* (Protective Squad), or SS. The SS would grow to become Hitler's private army and, on his orders, would carry out the bulk of the greatest crimes in the history of humanity—the crimes later known as the Holocaust.

In 1923, however, the Holocaust lay far in the future. Instead of millions of followers, Hitler could boast of only a few hundred, but among them were those who would be his closest lieutenants as he rose to supreme power. Ernst Röhm had been an officer in World War I, and his love of violence made him a natural choice for commander of the SA. Rudolf Hess had dropped out of college to join the *Freikorps* and distribute anti-Semitic propaganda. Alfred Rosenberg, who wrote that everything

noble in the world was due to the efforts of the Aryan race and that everything corrupt was the work of the Jews, was considered the Nazi philosopher. Julius Streicher was a violent, sadistic anti-Semite who published

Rudolf Hess (top) and Julius Streicher were two of Hitler's closest lieutenants during his rise to power.

an influential newspaper that luridly pictured Jews as rapers of Aryan women and murderers of Christian infants. Hermann Göring, who would become second only to Hitler in power, had been one of Germany's most-decorated pilots in World War I. He was rare among the early Nazis in that he had wealth and culture. He used his position in society to introduce Hitler to many influential people who contributed money to the Nazi cause.

A decorated fighter pilot in World War I, Hermann Göring would eventually become second only to Hitler in power.

In the fall of 1923, Hitler thought the Nazis' hour had arrived. He joined with other right-wing groups to plan a *putsch* (armed revolt) to seize control of the government of Bavaria, then march to Berlin and overthrow the republic. On the night of November 8, Göring burst into the Bürgerbräukeller, a huge beer hall, leading twenty-five armed SA storm troopers. Hitler, who had been in the crowd listening to a political speech, jumped atop a table, fired a pistol in the air, and announced, "The national revolution has broken out. . . . This hall is occupied by six hundred armed men, and no one may leave it."[25]

A Failed Rebellion

Hitler forced the leaders of the Bavarian government into a side room where he made them promise to support his revolt. However, when Hitler left to join some other troops attacking an army barracks, the government leaders talked their captors into releasing them. They then renounced Hitler and began to rally loyal army troops.

The next morning Hitler and his lieutenants marched at the head of three thousand Nazis toward Munich's central plaza. They found their path blocked by a hundred police armed with rifles. As the Nazis drew closer, a shot was fired—from which side no one could tell. At once, volleys rang out from both sides. Göring fell, wounded in the thigh. Hitler was dragged down to the pavement, separating his shoulder as he fell. Nineteen Nazis were killed and dozens wounded. Hitler managed to scramble to safety and escaped in a Nazi car.

What came to be called the Beer-Hall Putsch had failed. Hitler, Röhm, and other top Nazis were arrested and charged with treason. Göring and Hess fled to Austria. The Nazi Party was banned, and it appeared that Hitler's career was at an end.

Hitler, however, turned the situation to his advantage. At his February trial, covered by newspapers throughout Germany and by several foreign correspondents, he turned the prisoner's dock into a podium, lashing out at the "November criminals," who had led to Germany's defeat in World War I. He freely admitted he wanted to become a dictator, saying that the man who feels called to save his country cannot wait to be asked, but must step forward out of a sense of duty. At the trial's end, he told the court:

This memorial is dedicated to the Nazis who died in the Beer-Hall Putsch. Although this attempt at rebellion failed, Hitler later was able to turn the incident to his advantage.

Gentlemen, judgment will not be passed on us by you; judgment will be passed on us by the eternal court of history. . . . That other court, however, will not ask: "Did you or did you not commit high treason?" That court will pass judgment on us . . . who as Germans wanted the best for their people and their country, who were willing to fight and die for it.[26]

Prison and *Mein Kampf*

Hitler emerged from the trial a hero. He was found guilty, but the sympathetic judges gave him the lightest sentence possible—five years with eligibility for parole in six months. Prison was anything but an ordeal for Hitler and the fellow Nazis sentenced with him. Guards were friendly. Sympathizers brought them food, wine, and fresh flowers.

While his comrades played soccer in the prison yard, Hitler used his time in prison to write a book in which he would set forth his entire philosophy and his aims for the German people. He wanted to call the book *Four and a Half Years of Struggle Against Lies, Stupidity, and Cowardice*. His publisher convinced him to shorten it to *Mein Kampf* (My Struggle).

Mein Kampf was the Nazi blueprint for the start of World War II. Germans, as the master race, have a right to the land occupied by inferior people, namely the Poles and Slavs to the east. As for the Jews, they are destroyers of culture and have no place in greater Germany.

Hitler was released from prison in December 1924. He had learned two important lessons. First, he would never align the Nazis with other groups and thus dilute their power. Second, he would not try to take control by force, but would do so through the ballot box. He said,

> Instead of working to achieve power by [force], we shall have to hold our noses and enter the Reichstag [Germany's legislative body] against the Catholic and Marxist deputies. If out-voting them takes longer than out-shooting them, at least the result will be guaranteed by their own Constitution.[27]

The Nazis had some success at the polls, but their message began to lose its effectiveness. Germany was recovering from World War I. Times were better. People

While in prison, Hitler wrote Mein Kampf, *in which he set forth his philosophy and his goals for Germany and its people.*

had jobs and food. They no longer listened to the Nazi message of discontent. More than 2 million people voted for Nazi candidates in 1924; only 810,000 in 1928.

Hitler was not discouraged. He was willing to wait. He knew the republic had only lukewarm support from the majority of Germans and was convinced his moment would come. Meanwhile, he reorganized the party from the bottom up. At the very top was Hitler, who carried the official title of *Führer*, or leader. The country was divided into thirty-six districts, or *Gaue*, each headed by a *Gauleiter* answerable only to Hitler. The *Gaue* were further divided into *Kreise*, or circles, then into *Ortsgruppen*, or local groups. In cities, there were even neighborhood cells headed by a *Blockwart*, or block warden. Reporting directly to Hitler were several *Reichleiter*, or state leaders, who oversaw various departments.

Mein Kampf

Mein Kampf, the combined personal, philosophical, and political testament written by Hitler while he was in prison in 1924, became, almost literally, the bible of Nazi Germany. Alfred Rosenberg, chief "philosopher" of Nazism, wanted to place Hitler at the center of a new religion and substitute his book for the Bible.

While that idea never caught on with most Germans, *Mein Kampf* (My Struggle) nevertheless did become by far the best-selling book in Germany. After 1933 when the Nazis took power, it became the correct thing to do in German households to have a copy prominently displayed on a table or bookshelf. The book was also widely read outside Germany. By the end of World War II, *Mein Kampf* had sold more than 10 million copies in sixteen languages. Hitler's share of the book's sales brought him wealth, although personal wealth was something he cared nothing about.

Many Germans would admit in private that, while they owned *Mein Kampf,* they had never actually read it. Others would confess that they tried to read it but never got past the first few of its eight hundred pages. It was written in a dull, ponderous style and endlessly repeated the key themes of race, German destiny, survival of the fittest, and the need for a militaristic dictatorship.

While *Mein Kampf* may have been read outside Germany before Hitler took power, not enough people paid attention.

Robert Payne's evaluation, quoted in Yehuda Bauer's *A History of the Holocaust,* stated:

> There is no evidence that [Stanley] Baldwin, [Neville] Chamberlain, [Winston] Churchill, [Franklin] Roosevelt, [Josef] Stalin, or any of the political leaders most directly affected did anything more than glance at it. If they had read it with the attention it deserves, they would have seen that it was a blueprint for the total destruction of bourgeois [upper-middle-class] society and the conquest of the world.

Posters advertising Mein Kampf *cover a wall. Although it became the best selling book in Germany, relatively few people actually read it.*

An Unrepentant Hitler

When Adolf Hitler was imprisoned in 1924, various factions in the Nazi Party vied for power. Hitler purposely avoided taking sides so that no one could grow strong enough to take his place. As a result, the party was in almost total disarray when he was released.

On his release, he felt a need to publicly demonstrate that he was still in charge and that his program had not changed one bit, even in the wake of the failure of the Beer-Hall Putsch. On February 27, 1925, he spoke in the Bürgerbräukeller, the same beer hall in which he had declared a revolution in November 1923. He had promised the authorities of Bavaria that he would be moderate in his speaking. Either he had lied or he was swept away by the moment, because he was anything but moderate. This quote from the speech is taken from Alan Bullock's *Hitler: A Study in Tyranny*.

If anyone comes and wants to impose conditions on me, I shall say to him: "Just wait, my young friend, and see what conditions I impose on you." I am not contending for the favour of the masses. At the end of a year you shall judge, my comrades. If I have acted rightly, well and good. If I have acted wrongly, I shall resign my office into your hands. Until then, however, I alone lead the movement, and no one can impose conditions on me so long as I personally bear the responsibility. And I once more bear the whole responsibility for everything that occurs in the movement. . . . To this struggle of ours there are only two possible issues: either the enemy pass over our bodies or we pass over theirs, and it is my desire that, if in the struggle I should fall, the Swastika banner shall be my winding sheet.

This was too much for the officials of Bavaria. Hitler was forbidden to speak in public and was threatened to be imprisoned again if he ignored the ban.

Also reporting directly to Hitler were the military arms of the party, the SA and the SS.

A Parallel Society

At the same time the Nazis were streamlining their organization, they were bringing more groups of people under the party umbrella. Hitler's idea was to create a parallel society, with Nazism reaching into every aspect of German life. For young boys and girls, a *Jugendbund,* or youth association, was formed, later to be known as the Hitler Youth. There were other organizations for college students, pupils in elementary schools, teachers, and housewives.

The Nazis also reached into the professions, creating organizations for doctors, lawyers, civil servants, and artists.

Although they were not yet successful at the polls, the Nazis maintained a high degree of visibility throughout Germany. Their annual party rallies at Nuremberg drew tens of thousands to the spectacles over which Hitler presided like an emperor. Most German cities were witness to parades of SA men, their torches lighting the night sky, their boots pounding a rhythm on the pavement.

Hitler's waiting paid off. The crash of the American stock market in October 1929 brought an abrupt end to German prosperity, which had been propped up by foreign loans. Banks and businesses failed. Millions lost their jobs. The people were miserable, but Hitler was not. "Never in my life have I been so well disposed and inwardly contented as in these days," he wrote. "For hard reality has opened the eyes of millions of Germans." [28]

The president of Germany at the time was Paul von Hindenburg, an aging war hero, but the government was actually run by the chancellor, Hermann Müller. The military, concerned that Müller was too weak to prevent a Communist takeover, convinced Hindenburg to force Müller to resign and to appoint Heinrich Brüning chancellor. Brüning tried to combat economic troubles through a combination of higher taxes and budget cuts, but his program was assailed by both the Nazis on the right and the Communists on the left.

Article 48

Brüning realized he could not get the support of a majority in the Reichstag. He urged Hindenburg to invoke Article 48 of the Constitution that gave the chancellor the power to govern by executive decree in an emergency, without the consent of the Reichstag. The first step had been taken toward the destruction of democracy in Germany.

In the election of 1930, the Nazis polled 6.4 million votes—18 percent of the

President Hindenburg (wearing spiked helmet) sits with Hitler during a public ceremony. Hindenburg was unimpressed by the "Bohemian corporal"

total—and became the Reichstag's second-largest party. Hitler set out to dispel his reputation as a radical rabble-rouser. He increased his efforts to win the support of businessmen. He wooed the military, saying that Germany must have a strong army and that he had no intention of replacing the army with the SA, as some generals had feared.

In October 1931, Hitler met with Hindenburg for the first time. The aristocratic old soldier was unimpressed, sneering to others that this "Bohemian corporal"[29] would never be chancellor. Nevertheless, to try to keep the government out of Hitler's hands, Hindenburg decided to run in 1932 for another seven-year term as president. After a long deliberation, Hitler challenged him. Hindenburg won, but only after a runoff with Hitler.

Hindenburg blamed Brüning for Hitler's strong showing. An army spokesman, General Kurt von Schleicher, a close friend of Hindenburg's son, persuaded the president to replace Brüning with Franz von Papen as chancellor. The army thought Papen could be controlled, and Hitler supported the appointment because Papen promised to lift the ban on the SA that had been instituted by Brüning.

In the national elections on July 31, 1932, the Nazis replaced the Social Democrats as the largest party, winning 230 seats in the Reichstag—still short of a majority. Hitler once more tried to convince Hindenburg to appoint him chancellor. Hindenburg refused.

By November, Papen had resigned as chancellor, unable to build a majority from among the various parties. Schleicher persuaded Hindenburg to name him chancellor, convincing the president that he was the only one who could form a majority government and control the Nazis. He tried to split the Nazi Party by naming as deputy chancellor Gregor Strasser, a Nazi who had remained in the party despite frequent disagreements with Hitler. The plan failed when Strasser declined to challenge Hitler and retired from politics.

Papen and Hitler

Papen, meanwhile, felt betrayed by Schleicher. He began plotting with Hitler to overthrow the new chancellor and regain his place. Papen managed to get the ear of Hindenburg and convince him that Schleicher was losing support. Finally, on January 28, 1933, when Schleicher asked Hindenburg to call new elections, Hindenburg refused. Schleicher resigned, and Papen was asked to form a new government.

Papen knew that Hitler would not settle for anything less than chancellor. Hindenburg was opposed. Just a week earlier he had told a group of army officers, "Gentlemen, surely you do not think that I would appoint this Austrian corporal Chancellor of Germany?"[30] Papen, however, was persuasive. He argued that no government could succeed without Nazi support. He said that he, Papen, would be deputy chancellor and that only three members of the eleven-member cabinet would be Nazis.

Hindenburg finally gave in. At 11 A.M. on January 30, 1933, Hitler was summoned to the presidential palace. His Nazi lieutenants waited nervously in a nearby hotel. Would they be disappointed again? Joseph Goebbels, a party leader who would later become Hitler's minister of propaganda, wrote in his diary,

> What is happening there? We are torn between doubt, hope, joy and despair. We have been deceived too often to be able whole-heartedly to believe in the great miracle. . . . We shall be able to judge by his face if the interview was happy. . . . At last a car draws up in front of the entrance. . . . A few moments later he is with us. He says nothing, and we all remain silent also. His eyes are full of tears. It has come! The Führer is appointed chancellor.[31]

In less than a decade this former vagrant had gone from being convicted of treason against Germany to being appointed to the leadership of the country. Hitler now had the supreme power he had long sought. Both Germany and the rest of the world would soon learn how he planned to use it.

Chapter 3

The Nazification of Germany

Once Adolf Hitler became chancellor of Germany in January 1933, he wasted no time in consolidating his power and making the Nazi Party the dominant force in German politics. He was not content, however, to stop there. Between 1933 and the outbreak of World War II in 1939, Nazism would penetrate every aspect of German life and become interwoven in the fabric of the country.

Hitler's first step was to take complete control of the government. The Nazis were the largest party in the Reichstag, but had found it necessary to form a partnership with the National People's Party in order to have a voting majority. Only a week after becoming chancellor, Hitler convinced President Hindenburg to call new elections for March 5.

A week before the election, the Reichstag building was destroyed by fire. A Dutch Communist, Martin van der Lubbe, was arrested on the scene, and Hitler used the incident to persuade Hindenburg to sign an emergency decree suspending constitutional liberties. Thousands of Communists were jailed. Rallies of other political parties were broken up by Röhm's storm troopers and a new police unit, the *Geheime Staatspolizei* (Secret State Police), soon to become known as the Gestapo. Despite the week of terror, the Nazis still failed to get a majority, winning only 44 percent of the vote.

Hitler knew he would have to find a way to achieve absolute power without going to the voters. On March 23, the Reichstag met to consider the "Law for Removing the Distress of People and Reich," also known as the Enabling Act. This legislation took all authority away from the Reichstag and placed it with the cabinet. Hitler, as chancellor, would have the power to write all laws. A two-thirds vote of the Reichstag was necessary to pass the act, but this was no problem for the Nazis, who arrested all the Communist delegates and intimidated others. Within a few months, all state governments in Germany had been dissolved, labor unions had been outlawed, and a new law proclaimed that "The National Socialist German Workers' Party constitutes the only political party in Germany."[32]

Revolt in the Ranks

Hitler was now absolute master of Germany, but faced trouble within his own party. Röhm saw the Nazi revolution as having only just begun. He wanted to strip away the power of the major industrialists, break up large estates, and make the army subordinate to his SA. Hitler disagreed. He still needed the backing of the military and industry.

In June 1934 the two Nazi leaders had a bitter argument. Two days later, Röhm said publicly that "The SA is and remains the destiny of Germany."[33] Hitler took quick action to avert a civil war. On the morning of June 30, he confronted Röhm

and accused him of treason. He offered his old friend a choice—suicide or execution. Röhm refused to kill himself, and two SS officers did it for him.

Röhm was by no means the only one to die. Hitler took the opportunity to wipe out all opposition. An estimated eighty-five people were murdered and hundreds imprisoned on what came to be known as the Night of the Long Knives, or the Blood Purge. Among those killed were Gregor Strasser, whose ideas had long differed from Hitler's, and former chancellor Kurt von Schleicher.

At the same time Hitler was making himself absolute ruler of Germany, he was

Once Hitler became master of Germany, he moved quickly to eliminate those who opposed him. Two of his victims were former chancellor Kurt von Schleicher (Inset) and Ernst Röhm.

taking steps to make Nazism not merely a political philosophy, but a complete way of life. No aspect of society was too large or too small. Nothing was sacred, not even the family.

The Nazis demanded loyalty and obedience, and the traditional structure of the German family was ideal for their purposes. The German father was absolute master of his household, receiving unconditional obedience from his children and from his wife, at least in front of others. His role was that of breadwinner. His wife's was to bear children and care for the home. The children were to be obedient and work hard to make their parents proud.

The role of women in Nazi Germany ran counter especially to what was taking place elsewhere in western Europe and in the United States, where women were entering new professions and seeking the right to vote. The Nazis considered women little more than baby factories. As Joseph Goebbels said,

> The mission of women is to be beautiful and to bring children into the world. . . . The female bird pretties herself for her mate and hatches the eggs for him. In exchange, the mate takes care of gathering the food, and stands guard and wards off the enemy.[34]

The Exclusion of Women

In the Nazi view, a woman's place was in the home and nowhere else. Women were excluded by law from the legal profession, barred from serving on juries, and actively discouraged from careers in teaching or medicine. Hitler said,

> If today a female jurist accomplishes ever so much and next door there lives a mother with five, six, seven children . . . then I would like to say: From the standpoint of eternal value of our people the woman who has given birth to children and raised them . . . has accomplished more and does more.[35]

Marriage and large families were actively encouraged by vigorously persecuting homosexuals, banning abortion, and offering financial incentives for couples to have more children.

The Nazis did not hold such views out of a strong belief in the family. Indeed, the party did not want strong family ties because in Nazi Germany all loyalty was owed to the state and the *Führer.* The idea was to produce more future workers, mothers, and soldiers.

The Nazis wanted children to be obedient, but to the state, not necessarily to their parents. Organizations established for children and young people were designed to lessen family loyalties and bind them ever closer to the state. Boys ages ten to fourteen were to join the German Young Folk, and girls went into the League for Young Girls. From ages fifteen to eighteen, boys were in Hitler Youth and girls in the League of German Girls. The purpose was clear: to cap-

Hitler's Women

So dedicated was Adolf Hitler to what he considered his destiny as savior of Germany that he denied himself the pleasures of ordinary living. He wanted nothing—including a family—to distract him from his life's work. Once, while watching the children of Joseph Goebbels at play, he remarked how much he enjoyed children and how sad it was that it was his fate never to be a father.

Hitler's self-denial extended, for most of his life, to relationships with women. In addition to his conviction that all of his efforts should go to his work, he was painfully shy. However, there were two women—besides the beautiful Stefanie he had fantasized about as a youth—with whom he formed an attachment.

The first was his niece, a daughter of his half sister Angela Raubal. In 1925, Angela became Hitler's housekeeper and brought her daughters Geli and Friedl with her. Hitler was smitten with the seventeen-year-old Geli, who became his constant companion. Eventually, however, Hitler became overly possessive and refused to let Geli go out on her own. In September 1931, after a particularly stormy argument, Geli committed suicide. Hitler was grief-stricken and thought of committing suicide himself. He kept a picture of Geli in his room until the day he died, and she is probably the only woman he truly loved.

Hitler would eventually have a mistress, a charming, athletic young woman named Eva Braun. She was working in a photographer's shop when Hitler met her, and in the summer of 1932 she moved into his house. She ran his household and acted as hostess when he entertained friends and party cronies, but she was rarely seen with him in public and never accompanied him to state dinners or receptions.

Most observers thought there was nothing of a sexual nature between Hitler and Eva Braun and were astounded when, at the very end of World War II, the two were married in a bunker deep under Berlin as Russian artillery shells crashed overhead. The day after their marriage, they committed suicide together. Even though Eva Braun was Hitler's companion for more than thirteen years, there is no evidence that he had the deep emotional feeling for her that he had had for Geli Raubal.

Hitler and his mistress, Eva Braun. Hitler formed emotional attachments with only three women during his lifetime.

ture the hearts and minds of entire generations of young people. Hitler said, "When an opponent declares, 'I will not come over to your side,' I calmly say, 'Your child belongs to us already. . . . What are you? You will pass on. Your descendants, however, now stand in the new camp.'" [36]

The Nazis were interested in training both the minds and bodies of young people. Children were bombarded with

Hitler poses with the members of a German farmer's family, several of whom have dressed in uniform for the chancellor.

propaganda extolling the virtues of Hitler and the party. A tremendous emphasis was placed on physical fitness in order to prepare girls for motherhood, boys for war. Hitler Youth activities were highly militaristic. The importance the Nazis placed on the organization is reflected in its growth—from 107,956 members in 1933 to more than 8,800,000 in 1939.

Nazi Education

Along the same lines, the Nazis took firm control of education in Germany. Control of schools was removed from the states and placed with the Reich minister of education, Bernhard Rust. Courses were changed to fit Nazi doctrine. History was rewritten to portray Germans as the master race. Literature concentrated on heroic epics and legends. Courses in "racial science" were introduced, and efforts were made to teach "German" science and "German" mathematics. Students were supposed to absorb facts and parrot them back to their teachers. Independent thought and reasoning were discouraged, since they might lead students to question the state.

In addition to taking over the existing schools, the Nazis set out to create an entirely new system designed to prepare men, and a very few women, to be future party leaders. The National Political Institutes of Education ("Napolas") were modeled on military academies, with classes called "platoons." Students were educated in the "soldierly spirit," with heavy emphasis on physical fitness and political indoctrination.

The Adolf Hitler Schools, founded in 1937, were designed strictly as leadership schools for Hitler Youth and enrolled boys as young as twelve. The curriculum consisted principally of military training and Nazi ideology. After six years, graduates of the Adolf Hitler Schools were eligible to enter a university or military officer training.

A third type of school, the *Ordensburg* (Order Castle), was designed for the cream of Nazi youth. There were four castles, and students attended each one over a period of six years. One specialized in "racial science," a second in physical activities, a third in political and military instruction, and a fourth specifically in the Nazi doctrine of *Lebensraum*, seeking to take over lands to the east. Many graduates of the *Ordensburgen* later became SS officers and participated in the Holocaust.

In their efforts to dominate areas of society that influenced people's thoughts and emotions, the Nazis sought, as did the Communists in the Soviet Union, to stifle Christianity. Nazism would be the new religion. Christianity, with its emphasis on compassion, tolerance, and forgiveness, was completely at odds with Nazi goals. Besides, the Nazis said, Christianity was an offshoot of the hated Judaism. Christianity would be tolerated, but so bullied that it would reach the point, in Hitler's words, "where only complete idiots stand on the pulpit and preach to old women." [37] Nazi elements within the Christian churches sought to de-Christianize religious practices as much as they could by eliminating the celebration of traditional holidays. In 1938, for example, Christmas carols and Nativity plays were banned, and the word "Christmas" was officially replaced by "Yuletide."

Hitler poses with a member of the Hitler Youth. The Hitler Youth was part of a system designed to prepare young people to be future party leaders.

"God Believing"

The Nazi idea of religion was a faith called *Gottgläubig,* or "God Believing." Embraced by the most fanatical Nazis, this belief in effect substituted Hitler for Jesus, the idea being that God sent Hitler to save Germany. The Bible would be replaced by *Mein Kampf,* and the swastika would take the place of the cross on the altar.

The idea of *Gottgläubig* never caught on among the vast majority of the German people, who either remained aloof from religion entirely or stayed faithful to the two major denominations, Lutheran and Roman Catholic. Some elements of the Lutheran Church at first welcomed the Nazis but later rejected them. They fought efforts to de-Christianize the church and, led by Pastor Martin Niemöller, formed the Confessional Church, which actively opposed the Nazis. Niemöller and hundreds of other clergymen were eventually arrested and sent to concentration camps where many died.

The Roman Catholics, as members of a large, international church, were more difficult for the Nazis to intimidate. Indeed, when Hitler was seeking votes in the Reichstag for the Enabling Act in 1933, he courted the Catholic Center Party, promising not to interfere in church affairs. That July, the Nazi government signed an agreement with the international Roman Catholic Church in which it guaranteed the right of the church to govern itself.

Later, however, when German Catholic priests protested Nazi racial laws and the forced sterilization of the mentally retarded, Hitler ignored the agreement. One of the principal protesters, Erich Klausener, was murdered during the Blood Purge. Hundreds of priests and nuns were convicted on trumped-up charges of immorality and shipped to concentration camps. Catholic publications were suppressed.

The Nazis failed to eliminate the Christian churches of Germany, but they succeeded in silencing them. Once the church leaders were jailed, few came forth to take their places. Although there were acts of bravery by individual clergymen, the Lutheran and Roman Catholic Churches, as institutions, knuckled under to Nazi terror and failed to exert all their influence to prevent the crimes that would occur during World War II.

The Cultural Arena

The Nazis also sought to put their stamp on the cultural life of Germany. This arena especially interested Hitler, who was often bored with economics and the other day-to-day aspects of government but who still fancied himself an artist and architect. He immediately rejected the cultural establishment that had rejected him years before in Vienna. Anything modern or innovative was labeled "degenerate." As Hitler said in a speech opening the House of German Art in 1937,

Works of art that cannot be understood but need a swollen set of instructions to prove their right to exist and find their

Although classical architecture was the Nazi ideal, the style of public buildings such as the House of German Art (pictured) was instead cold, impersonal, and overpowering.

way to neurotics who are receptive to such stupid or insolent nonsense will no longer openly reach the German nation. Let no one have illusions! National Socialism has set out to purge the German Reich and our people of all those influences threatening its existence and character. . . . With the opening of this exhibition has come the end of artistic lunacy and with it the artistic pollution of our people.[38]

Art, in the Nazi view, was supposed to reflect the nobility of the German spirit. Paintings mostly centered on German legends or pictured the ideal Aryans—tall, bronzed, blond men and women working in fields or in domestic settings. The overriding theme was *Blut und Boden* (Blood and Soil), a rejection of urbanization and modernization and a glorification of the simple, conservative life.

Nazi architecture, on the other hand, was far from simple. Hitler personally drew up plans for a new capitol, a building that would include a domed meeting hall capable of holding 125,000 people. Any design remotely modern was out of the question. The architecture of ancient Greece and Rome was the Nazi ideal, but Hitler's architects failed to capture the spirit of classical architecture and instead designed a series of cold, impersonal buildings that conveyed a sense of raw power instead of beauty.

Literature

The *Blut und Boden* theme was extended to literature as well. Many leading writers left Germany shortly after the Nazis took power. One of these, Thomas Mann, later said, "It may be superstitious belief, but in my eyes, any books which could be printed at all in Germany between 1933 and 1945 are worse than worthless and not objects one wishes to touch. A stench of blood and shame attaches to them."[39] Most books revolved around four themes—war, race, the fatherland, and Nazism—and described the heroism of the German warrior, the triumph of German blood, the need to protect the sacred soil from Communists and Jews, and the role of Hitler as the great deliverer.

Not only were writers who deviated from the party line prohibited from publishing, but much of what they had already published was destroyed. On May 10, 1933, the German Student Union, actively encouraged by the Nazis, conducted a *Säuberung*, or "cleansing action," to rid the country of what it considered un-German writings. In cities throughout the country, students marched in torchlight parades to the central plazas. There they made huge bonfires out of the works of such German

Students burn "un-German" books during the Säuberung. Only works that dealt with war, race, the fatherland, and Nazism were considered acceptable.

writers as Mann and Albert Einstein, and such foreign authors as Jack London, Upton Sinclair, and H. G. Wells. Virtually all works by Jewish writers went into the flames, just as music by Jewish composers such as Felix Mendelssohn disappeared from music stores and concert halls.

As in any dictatorship, the Nazis held strict control over newspapers, radio, and motion pictures, and—as with education, religion, and culture—turned these means of information into tools of the government. Journalists had to be, by law, German citizens of Aryan descent. Editors of major newspapers in Berlin met daily with Joseph Goebbels, who ordered exactly what was and was not to be written. Similar instructions were telegraphed to other

Propaganda

One of the reasons for the Nazis' success was their ability to control the means of communication—radio, newspapers, books, motion pictures—and their skill at using them. Indeed, it is largely because of the Nazis that the word "propaganda"—meaning the systematic dissemination of information reflecting the views and interests of those advocating a doctrine or cause—took on a negative meaning.

In Joachim Fest's *The Face of the Third Reich,* Hitler is quoted on how a message must be repeated over and over to become successful propaganda:

> The chief function is to convince the masses, whose slowness of understanding needs to be given time in order that they may absorb information; and only constant repetition will finally succeed in imprinting an idea on their mind. Every digression in a propagandist message must always emphasize the same conclusions. The slogan must of course be illustrated in many ways and from several angles, but in the end one must always return to the assertion of the same formula. . . . The success of any advertisement, whether of a business or political nature, depends on the consistency and perseverance with which it is employed.

Some Nazi propaganda, such as the almost pornographic depictions of Jews, was extremely crude. Some was sophisticated. It didn't matter, Joseph Goebbels wrote in this quote from Fest's book, as long as it worked:

> That propaganda is good which leads to success, and that is bad which fails to achieve the desired result, however intelligent it is, for it is not propaganda's task to be intelligent, its task is to lead to success. Therefore no one can say your propaganda is too rough, too mean; these are not criteria by which it may be characterized. It ought not to be decent, nor ought it to be gentle or soft or humble; it ought to lead to success. If someone says to me, "Your propaganda is not at a well-bred level," there is no point in my talking to him at all. Never mind whether propaganda is at a well-bred level; what matters is that it achieves its purpose.

This crude anti-Semitic cartoon from a schoolbook portrays Jews as being immoral and profane.

newspapers throughout Germany. Those that did not comply were shut down or forced to sell out to more obedient rivals.

The Nazis were the first government to see the great propaganda possibilities of radio and motion pictures and to use them effectively. Radios were mass-produced and made as inexpensive as possible so that more Germans could own them. Loudspeakers were put in factories and in meeting halls so that people could gather to hear Nazi pronouncements preceded by blaring trumpet fanfares. As with the press, Goebbels's propaganda office strictly controlled the content of newscasts.

Motion Pictures

Many motion pictures, like literature and art, reflected conservative themes and glorified Hitler and the Nazis. Biographies of martyred storm troopers and stories of the heroic German soldiers of World War I were common. One film was so violently anti-Semitic that a Jewish man in Vienna was trampled to death by a Hitler Youth group that had recently seen it. Even the Nazis, however, realized the need for the masses to be entertained. Goebbels therefore gave producers and directors broad latitude in filming romances and comedies, just so long as they stayed away from politics.

The ultimate goal of Hitler and the Nazis was to make German society into a Nazi society. In addition to the youth groups, there were organizations for virtually every segment of society. The state, as embodied in the *Führer*, was everything; the individual, nothing. Individuality, both in action and thought, was frowned upon. Hitler wanted a nation of pliant, unthinking robots, blindly obedient to his will. In large measure, he succeeded, and the German people, arms raised in salute and shouting "*Heil*, Hitler," followed him down the road to war and destruction.

Chapter 4

The Fate of the Jews

From its birth in Munich to its death throes at the end of World War II, the Nazi Party was grounded on one fundamental concept—*Übermenschen* and *Üntermenschen*, the "superman" Germans and the "subhuman" Jews. Indeed, historian Klaus Fischer called anti-Semitism "the hate that fueled the Nazi movement."[40] Once the Nazis gained control and were able to turn the entire machinery of the state against their avowed enemies, Germany's Jews found their property, their rights, and eventually their lives in peril.

German anti-Semitism was by no means a Nazi invention. As far back as the Middle Ages, angry mobs, sometimes encouraged by priests who preached that the Jews bore responsibility for the crucifixion of Jesus, went on rampages through Jewish ghettos. During these wild uprisings, known as pogroms, Jewish shops and homes were looted and hundreds of Jews were beaten and killed.

The plight of German Jews was made even worse in the sixteenth century by Martin Luther, the man who began the

The Nazis did not invent German anti-Semitism. Martin Luther (pictured) turned against the Jews when they rejected his views of Christianity.

Protestant break from the Roman Catholic Church. Luther believed that the Jews had been correct to reject what he considered the false doctrines of Catholicism. When they also rejected his views of Christianity, Luther turned against them. "I cannot convert the Jews," he wrote. "Our Lord Christ Himself did not succeed in doing so: but I can close their mouths so that there will be nothing for them to do but lie upon the ground."[41]

In the eighteenth century, most German philosophers rejected the intellectual movement known as the Enlightenment, which held that people are shaped by observation and experience. The Germans thought instead that people were guided by an inborn spirit derived from their ethnic "blood."

Later, in the nineteenth century, when naturalist Charles Darwin wrote that species tend to survive because of advantageous traits inherited from previous generations, German philosophers were among those who applied Darwin's theories to humans. "Social Darwinism," which had little to do with Darwin's original conclusions, claimed that ethnic groups were in competition for dominance and that only the strongest and most pure would rule.

The *Volk*

Such views spawned the *völkisch* movement, of which the Thule Society, a forerunner of the Nazis, was a part. It was the destiny of the *Volk*—meaning all Germans, but in a tribal rather than national sense—to rule the world because of their pure "Aryan" blood. The chief corrupters of Aryan blood, in the *völkisch* view, were the Jews. It was not the Jewish religion that threatened the *Volk*, but the Jews themselves.

Hitler's Earliest Views on Race

On September 16, 1919, five years before *Mein Kampf* was written and only four days after Hitler attended his first meeting of the German Workers' Party—the small group that would later become the Nazi Party under his leadership—he wrote this view of the Jews in a letter. It is the earliest existing written expression of his racial philosophy and is quoted in *The Face of the Third Reich* by Joachim Fest:

Through a thousand years of incest, often practiced within the narrowest circles, the Jew has generally preserved his race and its characteristics more sharply than many of the peoples among whom he lives. His power is the power of money, which multiplies in his hands effortlessly and endlessly in the form of interest and imposes upon the peoples that most dangerous yoke, whose original golden gleam makes it so difficult to foresee its later melancholy consequences. Everything which makes man strive for higher things, whether it is religion, socialism or democracy, is to him all a means to the end of satisfying his lust for money and power. In their consequences his activities become a racial tuberculosis of the peoples. And this has the following result: anti-Semitism for purely emotional reasons will find its final expression in the form of pogroms [anti-Jewish riots]. The anti-Semitism of reason, however, must lead to the systematic combatting and elimination of Jewish privileges. Its ultimate goal must implacably be the total removal of the Jews.

To the Nazis, then, the Jews were a sub-human species that could not be permitted to pollute Aryan blood. To prevent them from doing so, they had to be set apart from German society. Eventually, the Nazis reached the conclusion that the only way to rid themselves of the Jewish threat was to murder all the Jews.

When Hitler became chancellor in 1933, the SA and SS began cracking down on Nazi opponents, among whom were many leaders of the Jewish community. Thousands were arrested without trial and packed into concentration camps such as Dachau, Buchenwald, and Bergen-Belsen, where many died of beatings and starvation. Horrible as they were, these camps were not designed for mass murder as were the later death camps in Poland, such as Auschwitz-Birkenau and Treblinka.

When the violence toward the Jews was condemned by foreign governments, Hitler was convinced the criticism was an international Jewish plot. He decided to call for an April 1 nationwide boycott of all Jewish businesses, but had not realized that such a boycott would also hurt German businesses that depended on Jewish firms for parts and supplies. Against the advice of his economists, he went ahead with the boycott, but so few people participated that it was called off in a few hours.

Undaunted, the Nazis next began enacting a series of laws aimed at removing Jews as an integral part of German society. Starting in April 1933, legislation banned Jews from the civil service, teaching, law,

medicine, the arts, and journalism. In September, they were prevented from holding any government job.

The first step toward achieving "racial purity" was taken in July 1933 with passage of the Entitled Law for the Prevention of Progeny with Hereditary Diseases. More than four hundred thousand persons—not only Jews, but also Gypsies and some Germans—were forcibly sterilized because of "undesirable" conditions ranging from mental retardation to homosexuality.

Jewish Reaction

The anti-Jewish laws of 1933 caused more than thirty-seven thousand Jews to flee Germany, but the overwhelming majority remained. Many Jewish families had been in Germany for centuries, and their members were prominent in their communities. They considered themselves Germans first and Jews second. Many others reasoned that the Nazis were nothing new. They were, after all, only one more affliction in a long history of tribulation and, like the others, would pass on, leaving the Jewish community intact.

Indeed, it seemed in 1934 as if the fears of the Jews had been overblown. Persecution diminished, and no new racial laws were passed. The Jews thought that perhaps the worst was over. They could not have been more wrong.

Hitler had been far too occupied with setting the Nazi house in order to pay much attention to the Jews. That would change dramatically with the passage of the

Nuremberg Laws, so called because they were presented at the annual Nazi rally in Nuremberg on September 15, 1935. These

United in Danger

Jews had lived in Germany well over a thousand years before Adolf Hitler and the Third Reich. While there had been savage persecutions during the Middle Ages, more recent centuries had seen a great assimilation of Jews into German society. Many leading businessmen, scientists, artists, and educators were Jewish. They were leaders in their communities and considered themselves Germans first, Jews second.

The Nazis changed all such comfortable beliefs. The anti-Jewish laws of 1933 brought the Jews face-to-face with their religion and their ethnicity. The result was an awakening and strengthening of Jewish faith. Robert Wetsch, a leader of the German Zionists, an organization that advocated the Jews' return to a homeland in Palestine, wrote, as quoted in Yehuda Bauer's *A History of the Holocaust:*

> The first of April, 1933 [the date of a boycott of Jewish businesses], will remain an important date in the history of German Jewry—indeed, in the history of the entire Jewish people. . . . Today the Jews cannot speak except as Jews. Anything else is utterly senseless. . . . Gone is the fatal misapprehension of many Jews that Jewish interests can be pressed under some cover. . . . April 1, 1933, can become the day of Jewish awakening and Jewish rebirth. If the Jews will it. If the Jews are mature and have greatness in them. . . . A powerful symbol is to be found in the fact that the boycott leadership gave orders that a sign "with a yellow badge on a black background" was to be pasted on the boycotted shops. This regulation is intended as a brand, a sign of contempt. We will take it up and make of it a badge of honor.

two laws gave legal status to the Nazi view of Jews as racially inferior and attempted to permanently define their status within German society.

The first law, the Law for the Protection of German Blood and German Honor, forbade both marriage and sexual relations between Jews and non-Jewish Germans and banned the employment in Jewish homes of any German female under forty-five years of age. The second law, the Reich Citizenship Law, denied German citizenship to Jews and gave them instead the status of "subjects."

Two months later, a decree from Hitler spelled out exactly who, in the Nazis' opinion, was a Jew. A "full Jew" was deemed to be anyone descended from three or more Jewish grandparents, or anyone with two Jewish grandparents who either practiced the Jewish religion, was married to a Jew, or had been born after June 15, 1935, to one Jewish parent and one non-Jewish German parent. Other part-German, part-Jewish people were labeled *Mischlinge*, or half-breeds, and denied rights of full citizenship. Jews were made to wear identifying badges—a yellow Star of David.

The Jews of Germany had widely varying reactions to the Nuremberg Laws. Many could now see that the Nazi persecution was to be unlike anything known before. Twenty-one thousand Jews emigrated from Germany in 1935 and twenty-five thousand in 1936. On the other hand, many other Jews felt a sense of relief in that the new laws at least let them know where they stood. One group called the laws "a basis that will enable tolerable relations to develop between the German nation and the Jewish nation."[42]

An Outcast People

Meanwhile, Goebbels's propaganda machinery and violent attacks in Streicher's newspaper were having the desired effect on the German people. Jews, already banned from holding many kinds of jobs, now began to experience severe discrimination outside the workplace as well. They were refused entry into restaurants and other businesses. Benches in parks were labeled either "No Jews" or "Jews Only." Anti-Semitic graffiti appeared on walls and on the windows of Jewish shops. Jews found themselves shunned by people who only a few months before had been good friends.

How much actual anti-Jewish feeling existed in Germany is difficult to say. Many Germans avoided the Jews out of fear instead of hate. Supporting the Jews in any way became a criminal offense that would leave non-Jews open to severe treatment by the secret police. Germany was rapidly becoming a police state. The Gestapo was

Anti-Semitic graffiti stains the window of a Jewish shop in Frankfurt. Jews also experienced discrimination outside of the workplace.

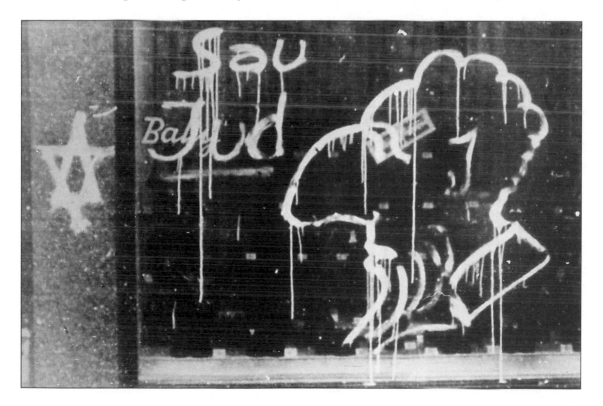

placed under Heinrich Himmler, who had been named by Hitler to head the SS in 1929. Under the leadership of this mild-looking but fanatical man, the Nazi police agencies would create a climate of fear throughout Germany and, during World War II, most of Europe. The investigative arm of the SS was the *Sicherheitsdienst* (SD), or security service, headed by Reinhard Heydrich. Both Himmler and Heydrich would play major roles in the Holocaust.

Other nations in Europe and throughout the world were increasingly critical of Hitler and the Nazis because of the anti-Jewish laws and the increasingly harsh way the Jews were treated. Hitler needed a way to show the world that stories of maltreatment of Jews were exaggerated. He also desired a public relations event that would trumpet the accomplishments of Nazism. The opportunity came with the 1936 Olympic Games in Berlin.

Heinrich Himmler questions a Jewish worker at a concentration camp during World War II.

Hitler made sure Germany presented its best face to the world's visitors at the Olympics. Anti-Jewish graffiti was removed, sometimes by the Jews themselves under the eyes of SS men. The yellow Stars of David disappeared. Anyone suspected of wanting to start a public protest was quietly arrested and sent to a concentration camp.

For the most part, Olympic visitors failed to see past the Nazi façade. Indeed, many who had seen the war-ravaged Germany of the early 1920s remarked on the positive changes brought about by Hitler's rule. To all outward appearances, people were industrious, happy, and content with their government. The visitors began to believe Hitler's claim that the stories of bad treatment of the Jews were nothing more than a plot by international Jewry.

The Four-Year Plan

Once the Olympic torch had been extinguished and the athletes and spectators departed, the façade crumbled. On September 9, 1936, Hitler announced a Four-Year Plan to reform the German economy. Göring was placed in charge. The intent was that "Germany must be wholly independent of foreign areas in those materials which can be produced in any way through German ability."[43] The public was told that the Four-Year Plan would improve the lot of the German worker. In reality, Hitler was already looking toward war and wanted to make Germany as self-sufficient as possible.

One aspect of the Four-Year Plan—not part of the public announcement—was Aryanization, a system to strip Jews of their property. Not only did this stop emigrating Jews from taking wealth out of the country, but it also lined the pockets of Hitler's top lieutenants. When Jewish business owners found it almost impossible to operate under the racial laws, they were offered an "opportunity" to sell their firms at a cut-rate price. Helpless, they agreed. Although the process was supposed to redistribute Jewish wealth among the German population, it really enriched the top Nazis, particularly Göring, and their friends. Hitler himself, however, was never interested in personal wealth but only in the "purification" of Germany.

In addition to losing their property, Jews who chose to leave Germany lost much of what little wealth they had left because of the "flight tax" imposed on them—normally one-fourth of all their assets. The flight tax enriched the Nazi treasury by the equivalent of $132 million in 1938 and 1939. Many Jews fleeing Hitler arrived at their destinations with little more than the clothing they wore. They did, however, have their lives, which was more than could eventually be said for those who remained.

As they had done throughout centuries of persecution and discrimination, the Jews adapted to changing events. Even though many fled their homeland, an estimated 392,000—three-fourths of the Jewish population in Germany in 1933—remained at the end of 1937. Perhaps they thought that, since they had survived the terrors and exclusionary laws of 1933, the racial laws of 1935, and the Four-Year Plan of 1937, they had weathered the storm and the worst was over. It was not.

Kristallnacht

On November 6, 1938, a German diplomat in Paris was shot dead by a Jew whose parents had been put in a concentration camp. The Nazis used the incident as an excuse to unleash a night of terror undreamed of by Germany's Jews. To the casual observer, the events of November 9 were spontaneous uprisings. In reality, they had been carefully planned by Goebbels and organized by Himmler and Heydrich.

That night, in cities throughout Germany, the SA and SS went on a rampage. Synagogues were burned to the ground. Hundreds of Jews were beaten, and at least thirty-six were killed. Thousands were dragged from their homes and shipped off to concentration camps. The windows of Jewish shops and homes were shattered and the contents looted. The streets of Jewish sectors were filled with so much broken

Germans pass by the broken shop window of a Jewish-owned business that was looted during Kristallnacht.

glass that the night came to be known as *Kristallnacht*, the Night of Broken Glass.

The arrests had not been random. Heydrich's instructions to the SS specified that "as many Jews, especially rich ones, are to be arrested as can be accommodated in the existing prisons."[44] The purpose of *Kristallnacht* had been twofold: to send an unmistakable message to the Jews that they were unwelcome in Germany, and to further swell the Nazi treasury. The Reichstag, presided over by Göring, carried out an "investigation" of the riots and laid the blame at the feet of the Jews! If insurance claims were paid, all money went to the government. In addition, the Jews of Germany were fined a billion marks for "their abominable crimes."[45]

By now, the Nazis had moved from a policy of separating the Jews from other Germans to doing everything in their power to drive them from the country altogether. *Kristallnacht* accelerated the process of emigration. In the year between *Kristallnacht* and the outbreak of World War II, another 100,000 Jews fled from Germany and another 116,000 emigrated from Austria, which had been annexed by the Nazis in March 1938.

Forced Emigration

For those Jews not frightened enough to leave Germany, a program of forced emigration was begun. The SS officer in charge of Section IV-B-4, "Jewish Affairs," was thirty-three-year-old Adolf Eichmann, later to become one of the principal per-

As head of the SS's "Jewish Affairs" section, Adolf Eichmann was in charge of the forced emigration of Jews who were not frightened enough to leave Germany.

petrators of the Holocaust. In 1938, however, Eichmann's job was not to kill Jews, but to strip them of all wealth possible and send them elsewhere. The difficulty was where to send them.

Many foreign governments, including Great Britain, France, and the United States, criticized Nazi Germany for its treatment of Jews. Accepting these Jews as immigrants, however, was another matter. Some countries feared that a wave of refugees would take jobs away from their own citizens. Others closed their borders to

Jews out of anti-Semitism. In July 1938, U.S. President Franklin Roosevelt called an international conference at Evian, France, to address the problem of Jewish refugees from Germany and Austria. Rather than saying what they would do for the Jews, most of the twenty-nine countries represented, including the United States, made it clear that they would not accept more Jews.

One of the havens for Jews was Palestine, which was controlled by Great Britain. About 171,000 Jews were admitted between 1933 and 1936. Arab leaders, however, pressured the British government into drastically limiting Jewish immigration late in 1936, and only about 25,000 were legally admitted in 1937 and 1938. Others were smuggled into Palestine illegally by the Zionist movement, which was committed to establishing a homeland for Jews worldwide.

Nazi policy toward the Jews seemed to proceed in stages. At first, Jews were stripped of their rights and wealth but allowed to remain in Germany as persecuted noncitizens. Later it was thought that the very presence of Jews might lead to a further corruption of Aryan blood, and the program of forced emigration was begun. With the outbreak of World War II in 1939, emigration was no longer an option and the Nazis had to look elsewhere than Western Europe and America for a place to send the Jews. Instead of west, they looked east to Poland.

The Euthanasia Program

In October 1939 Hitler had set out to cleanse Germany of "undesirables" such as the insane and physically deformed through a program of euthanasia, or "mercy" killings. Those selected, including many Jews falsely certified as insane, were taken to hospitals and put to death. Hitler's personal physician, Karl Brandt, along with euthanasia program director Philipp Bouhler, came up with the idea of executing their victims by gassing them in rooms disguised as shower baths. The program had to be discontinued in 1940 because of protests by German clergymen. The euthanasia program was eventually moved to Poland and grew into the Holocaust.

When Germany conquered and occupied the western half of Poland in 1939, the decision was made to build gigantic new labor camps there. In February 1940 the first major concentration camps, Belzec and Auschwitz, were established and the Jews of Germany and Austria began to be shipped there by the trainload, packed into cattle cars. Neither camp yet engaged in organized mass murder, but that was to come shortly.

Germany invaded the Soviet Union in June 1941, and squads of SS *Einsatzgruppen*, or action groups, followed in the wake of the troops, rounding up and shooting to death thousands of Soviet Jews. This method, the Nazis discovered, was costly and inefficient. Later in the summer, Göring ordered Heydrich to prepare a plan for "the Final Solution [*Endlösung*] of the Jewish question."[46] A few weeks later, Rudolf Hess, commandant of Auschwitz, was summoned to Berlin by Himmler and told:

Men certified as being "undesirable" await execution in a gas chamber somewhere in Poland. The chambers were usually disguised as shower baths.

The *Führer* [Hitler] has ordered that the Jewish question be solved once and for all and that we, the SS, are to implement that order. The existing exter-mination centers in the east [the *Einsatzgruppen*] are not in a position to carry out the large actions which are anticipated. . . . The Jews are the sworn enemies of the German people and must be eradicated.[47]

The progression of Nazi policy toward the Jews was now complete. In the end, Hitler considered the Jews such a danger

The *Einsatzgruppen*

Although most of the Jews were murdered in the death camps of Poland, the Holocaust did not begin there, but far to the east, in the western part of the Soviet Union known as Ukraine, where hundreds of thousands of Jews lived. Ukraine was one of the prime areas where Hitler sought *Lebensraum* (living space) for the German people. Naturally, according to his philosophy, it would have to be "cleansed" of Jews.

To accomplish this cleansing, special troops known as *Einsatzgruppen* (action groups), moved in behind the invading German army in June 1941. In this excerpt from *Foreign Policy, War, and Racial Extermination* by Jeremy Noakes and Geoffrey Pridham, SS officer David Ehof describes the procedure:

The condemned people were not only brought in lorries [trucks] but also on foot in groups of 70 or 80 persons and were mercilessly beaten in the process. The people who had been brought to the place of execution were placed about fifty metres [about 160 feet] from the graves and guarded until it was their turn to be shot. Twenty or twenty-five people at a time were led to the place of execution, to the graves. At the graves they were undressed; they even had their good quality underclothes torn from their bodies. Having been completely undressed they were driven to the graves and were forced to lie face down. The police and Germans shot them with rifles and automatic weapons. In this way more and more groups were driven to the graves and shot. They too were made to lie face down on the corpses of those who had been previously shot. At the place of exe-

cution there were snacks and schnapps [high-alcohol liquor]. The police drank schnapps and had a snack in the intervals between shooting the groups of Jews and then got back to their bloody work in a state of intoxication.

Members of an Einsatzgruppe *stand over their victims somewhere in the Ukraine. The condemned were usually made to lie down in their graves before being shot.*

to pure German blood that they had to be wiped off the face of the earth. Auschwitz and Belzec would be joined by four other death camps: Treblinka, Chelmno, Majdanek, and Sobibor. In them, separated from the outside world by World War II, about 6 million people would die in what has become known as the Holocaust.

Chapter 5

The Road to War: Weakness and Strength

Adolf Hitler had never made a secret of his ultimate vision for Germany. First, all peoples of German blood, the *Volk*, would be united into one *Reich*. Then, to acquire *Lebensraum*, or living space, for the *Volk*, territory to the east would be seized from Poland and the Soviet Union. It had all been set forth in *Mein Kampf*:

> The German people must be assured the territorial area which is necessary for it to exist on earth. . . . When we speak of new territory . . . we must principally think of Russia. . . . The territory on which one day our German peasantry will be able to bring forth and nourish their sturdy sons will justify the blood of the sons of the peasants that has to be shed today.[48]

Hitler's words, while widely read around the world, were little heeded. Other nations were so intent on peace that they did not try to stop the Nazi dictator until it was too late.

"They left us alone and let us slip through the risky zone,"[49] Goebbels crowed later.

Joseph Goebbels (seen here with Hitler) bragged that other nations left Germany alone in a futile effort to maintain peace.

By 1933, when the Nazis gained power, Germany had recovered much of its economic and industrial strength. Militarily, however, it was weak, still shackled by the provisions of the Treaty of Versailles. The army was limited to one hundred thousand men. The navy was limited to thirty-five ships, none of which was allowed to match those of the British and French in size and power. The *Luftwaffe* (air force) was abolished altogether. Hitler therefore had to prepare Germany for war while convincing the rest of the world he wanted nothing but peace. It is a tribute to both his diplomacy and his duplicity that he succeeded.

Hitler knew that his ultimate success depended on his ability to rearm Germany. He began laying the groundwork almost immediately after taking power. In a May 1933 speech, widely reported by the international press, he said, "Germany would be perfectly willing to disband her entire military establishment and destroy the small amount of arms remaining to her if the neighboring countries will do the same thing with equal thoroughness."[50]

He claimed that other European countries were bound by the Treaty of Versailles to disarm, and that, if they refused, Germany had a right to maintain equality. There was a measure of truth in what he said, since the treaty had called for "a general limitation of the armaments of all nations."[51] Hitler knew full well, however, that none of his neighbors would agree to any limitation, so he used it as an excuse for his next step.

Leaving the League

In October, he announced to the German people that he was bitterly disillusioned by other nations' failure to disarm. Their decision, he said sorrowfully, left him no choice but to pull Germany out of the League of Nations and to withdraw from the international disarmament talks under way in Geneva, Switzerland. He added, however, that he would be guided by the will of the German people and would put his decision to a popular vote. Not surprisingly, 95 percent of the voters in the Nazi-controlled election approved his actions.

A few months later, in January 1934, Hitler made the first of several shrewd moves designed to sow discord among European alliances by announcing a ten-year nonaggression treaty with Poland. This move appeared on the surface to be a peaceful gesture, as there was bitterness between the two countries over the Polish Corridor, a small strip of land connecting Poland to its seaport city of Danzig and separating East Prussia from the rest of Germany. Actually, however, it weakened the alliance between Poland and France, which looked toward the Poles as allies in the east if Germany ever attacked France. It also gave Poland a sense of security, a false one as it turned out. As Hitler told a confidant, "I have no intention of maintaining a serious friendship with Poland."[52]

The next move was in Austria, where the Nazis had been growing in strength and frightening the government with their demands for unity with Germany. In July,

The "New Order"

Hitler's ultimate dream was a world dominated by the master race—those of pure "Aryan" blood. In his view, national boundaries would become insignificant. Only ethnicity and racial purity would matter. He called his vision for the future the New Order and described it thus as quoted in Alan Bullock's *Hitler: A Study in Tyranny:*

> The conception of the nation has become meaningless. We have to get rid of this false conception and set in its place the conception of race. The New Order cannot be conceived in terms of national boundaries of the peoples with an historic past, but in terms of race that transcends these boundaries.... France carried her great Revolution beyond her borders with the conception of nation. With the conception of race, National Socialism will carry its revolution abroad and recast the world. I shall bring into operation throughout Europe and the whole world this process of selection which we have carried out through National Socialism in Germany.... The active sections in nations, the militant, Nordic section, will rise again and become the ruling element over these shopkeepers and pacifists, these puritans and speculators and busybodies.... There will not be much left then of the clichés of nationalism, and precious little among us Germans. Instead there will be an understanding between the various language elements of the one good ruling race.

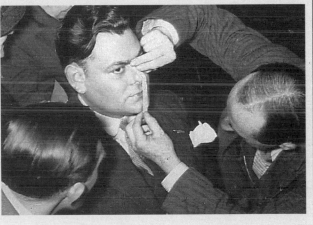

A German's nose is measured to determine his Aryan purity. Followers of the "New Order" believed that one's race could be determined by physical characteristics.

more than 150 Austrian Nazis broke into the Chancellery in Vienna and shot Chancellor Engelbert Dollfuss dead. They then broadcast that he had resigned and that they would form a new government. Several thousand storm troopers waited just across the German border, ready to assist their comrades.

For once, however, Hitler had overstepped himself. The minister of justice, Kurt von Schuschnigg, quickly marshaled loyal military forces and arrested the rebels. Also, Italian dictator Benito Mussolini massed troops on the Austrian border. Mussolini feared that if Hitler gained control of Austria, he might someday threaten to take over the South Tyrol, an area of far northern Italy where many people of German ancestry lived. Hitler knew he lacked the strength to challenge his Italian counterpart. He hastily withdrew a prepared announcement rejoicing in the merging of the two countries and substituted one professing outrage at the "cruel murder" of Dollfuss.[53]

The Saar Election

Hitler had failed to grab Austria by force, but he was soon to get a smaller prize by peaceful means. Since World War I, the Saar, a rich coal-mining region on the German-French border, had been under the control of the League of Nations. As called for by the Treaty of Versailles, an election was conducted on January 13, 1935, in which the people of the Saar voted overwhelmingly to rejoin Germany. To soothe the nervous French, Hitler proclaimed that "the Germans will make no further territorial claims on France,"[54] meaning that he renounced Germany's claims to the areas of Alsace and Lorraine, which had been ruled by Germany prior to World War I.

The French were not fooled. They took action to build up their army by lengthen-

ing the term of military service. This action only served to give Hitler an excuse for his next move, his boldest to date. In March, on a Saturday—Hitler's favorite day for surprise announcements—he proclaimed what much of the world already suspected: Germany had an air force. This was a direct violation of the Treaty of Versailles, but Hitler was not yet through. The following Saturday he announced that Germany would resume a military draft, and put the size of the army at thirty-six divisions—about half a million men.

The other nations reacted by convening a conference at Stresa on Lake Maggiore in Italy. Mussolini demanded action, but Great Britain clearly did not favor either military action or economic sanctions. Two leading British diplomats, John Simon and Anthony Eden, had visited Hitler in Berlin, where the Nazi leader made the persuasive claim that he was beefing up his army only to act as a barrier between the Communist Soviet Union and the rest of Europe. In the end, Britain, Italy, and France condemned Germany's violation of the Treaty of Versailles, as did the League of Nations, but nothing was done to correct it. Once more, Hitler had driven a small wedge between his opponents.

He was able to drive it deeper in May, giving another major speech intended to

German soldiers stand at attention at Nuremberg. Even though Hitler violated the Treaty of Versailles by rebuilding the army, Britain, France, and Italy did nothing.

calm his neighbors. Germany, he said, "wants peace . . . owing to the realization of the simple primitive fact that no war would be likely to alter the distress in Europe . . . whosoever lights the torch of war in Europe can wish for nothing but chaos."[55] He said that, as a gesture of peace, he would be willing to limit the German navy to 35 percent of the British navy. To the British, 35 percent sounded reasonable, and they negotiated a treaty to that effect with Hitler. To the French and Italian leaders, who had not been consulted, it was not reasonable at all because it allowed for a large German navy in further violation of the Treaty of Versailles.

Allying with Mussolini

Yet another opportunity to divide the European nations came in October 1935 when Mussolini, promising the Italian people a new Roman Empire, invaded the African nation of Ethiopia. Led by the demands of Britain and France, the League of Nations imposed economic sanctions on Italy. Hitler took the opportunity, while professing neutrality, to sell badly needed coal to Mussolini, thereby earning the Italian dictator's friendship and turning him away from Britain and France. It was a win-win situation for Hitler. In his diary, journalist William L. Shirer wrote,

> Either Mussolini will stumble and get himself so heavily involved in Africa that he will be greatly weakened in Europe, whereupon Hitler can seize Austria, hitherto protected by the Duce [Mussolini]; or he will win, defying France and Britain, and thereupon be ripe for a tie-up with Hitler against the Western democracies.[56]

With Italy fighting in Ethiopia and the attention of Britain and France turned to-

ward Africa, Hitler decided the time was right for his boldest move yet—the remilitarization of the Rhineland. Both the Treaty of Versailles and the Locarno Pact, which Germany had freely negotiated in 1925, mandated that this section of Germany on its border with France was to remain free of armed forces, but Hitler was determined to occupy it with his troops. His generals protested. They knew, as did Hitler, that the German army was still far too weak to stand up to the French. But would the French act? That was the key question.

The remilitarization of the Rhineland was a huge gamble, and Hitler knew it. The Nazi government depended on maintaining a perception of absolute power. "A retreat on our part," he said later, "would have spelled collapse."[57] He was betting, however, that the leaders of Britain and France would do almost anything to avoid war. He was right.

Winning the Gamble

Early on the morning of March 7, 1936, a small force of twenty-two thousand German troops marched into the Rhineland. As Hitler and his lieutenants waited nervously in Berlin, the French argued among themselves about how to react. The government wanted to send troops, but the French high command hesitated, even though it would have had overwhelming numerical superiority. In addition, the French government's resolve was not shared by Britain. One British diplomat, Lord Lothian, said, "The

Into the Rhineland

On March 7, 1936, Hitler sent German troops into the Rhineland, an area of Germany along the French border. This action was a direct violation of both the Treaty of Versailles of 1919 and the Locarno Pact, which Germany had freely signed in 1925, agreeing that this area was to remain demilitarized.

William L. Shirer, an American correspondent in Berlin, kept a diary during his seven years there. These passages from his book *Berlin Diary* give his reaction to the arming of the Rhineland and to the inaction of the French:

BERLIN, *March 7:* . . . After lunch I took a stroll alone through the Tiergarten to collect my thoughts. Near the Skagerakplatz I ran into General [Werner] von Blomberg walking along with two dogs on a leash. His face was still white, his cheeks twitching. "Has anything gone wrong?" I wondered. . . .

BERLIN, *March 8:* Hitler has got away with it!

France is not marching. Instead it is appealing to the League [of Nations]! No wonder the faces of Hitler and Göring and Blomberg and [General Werner von] Fritsch were all smiles this noon as they sat in the royal box at the State Opera. . . .

Oh, the stupidity (or is it paralysis?) of the French! I learned today on absolute authority that the German troops which marched into the demilitarized zone of the Rhineland yesterday had strict orders to beat a hasty retreat if the French army opposed them in any way. They were not prepared or equipped to fight a regular army. That probably explains Blomberg's white face yesterday. Apparently Fritsch (commander-in-chief of the Reichswehr [the German army]) and most of the generals opposed the move, but Blomberg, who has a blind faith in the Führer and his judgment, talked them into it.

Germans, after all, are only going into their own back garden."[58] In the end, Hitler won his gamble. The democracies did nothing, not realizing that their best—and possibly last—chance for preventing World War II had passed.

As Germany rebuilt its armed forces, it needed an opportunity to test equipment and tactics and season officers without actually going to war. The opportunity came only four months later when civil war broke out in Spain. General Francisco Franco, attempting to overthrow the republican government and establish a dictatorship, appealed to Mussolini and Hitler for help. Mussolini dispatched massive

military aid to Franco, but Hitler was more cautious. He sent one air force unit, the Condor Legion; a tank battalion; and a host of "technical advisers."

The Spanish Civil War lasted three years, during which the Germans learned much, including the effectiveness of a massive assault combining tanks and aircraft. They would later put these lessons to use with devastating effect during World War II.

The conflict in Spain had additional benefits for Hitler. Since Britain and France opposed a Franco takeover, Mussolini was further alienated from them. Hitler took full advantage of the shift in alliances to win as an ally the man who only

Hitler and His Generals

Hitler never liked or trusted the German military establishment. He thought they were too timid, too conservative. He also thought—rightly—that the generals, most of whom came from old, distinguished families, looked down on him as only a former corporal.

When Hitler sent troops into the Rhineland in 1936, his generals, led by Commander-in-Chief Werner von Fritsch, had opposed him but were talked into supporting the move by Defense Minister Werner von Blomberg. Both officers, however, were appalled when Hitler announced at a meeting on November 5, 1937, that he meant to annex Austria and Czechoslovakia and would go to war if he had to.

Sensing their disapproval, Hitler vowed to rid himself of both his top military leaders. The opportunity presented itself in January 1938. Hermann Göring and Heinrich Himmler, who disliked both Fritsch and Blomberg because they opposed the formation of combat SS battalions, informed Hitler that Blomberg's second wife, his former secretary, had once been a prostitute. The scandal caused Fritsch to ask Hitler to dismiss Blomberg.

Hitler not only dismissed Blomberg, but he also accused Fritsch of homosexual practices based on information Göring and Himmler had supplied. He brought the general face-to-face with his accuser, Hans Schmidt, an unsavory character who made his living blackmailing homosexuals. Schmidt positively identified Fritsch as one of his victims. The outraged Fritsch maintained a dignified silence, and Hitler sent him on indefinite leave, eventually naming a replacement for him.

Later, Fritsch was exonerated by an army court. The evidence, as was known by the

Hitler speaks with Werner von Blomberg (far left) and Werner von Fritsch. Hitler thought his generals to be cowardly and overcautious.

Gestapo all along, was false. It had been another officer, also named Fritsch, that had been Schmidt's victim, but Schmidt had agreed to cooperate with Göring and Himmler.

Both Fritsch and Blomberg remained in the army. Fritsch was killed in battle outside Warsaw, Poland, in 1939, and Blomberg died in an American prison in 1946.

two years earlier had called him a "dangerous fool."[59] In September 1937, Hitler invited Mussolini to make a state visit. No efforts were spared to impress and flatter the Italian leader. Military parades were held in his honor. He and Hitler spoke to a cheering open-air crowd of more than a million people. Hitler spoke of his fellow dictator as "one of those lonely men of the ages on whom history is not tested, but who themselves are the makers of history."[60] Mussolini was overwhelmed and, convinced that his destiny lay with Hitler's, agreed to join the Anti-Comintern Pact, a treaty between Germany and Japan signed the year before. The Rome-Berlin-Tokyo "Axis" was taking shape.

The Seizure of Austria

With Germany's military strength increasing, the western democracies paralyzed, and Mussolini won over, Hitler decided that the time was ripe for another move against Austria. In a speech on February 20, 1938, he told the Reichstag, "It is intolerable for a self-respecting world power to know that across the frontier are kinsmen who have to suffer. . . . To the interest of the German Reich belongs also the protection of those fellow-Germans who live beyond our frontiers."[61]

The Austrian Nazis, who

had gone underground after the failed *putsch* in 1934, had become active once more, committing increasingly frequent acts of terrorism during 1937. Their objective was to create a situation of such chaos that Germany would feel compelled to intervene to "restore order." The Austrian chancellor, Schuschnigg, could see what was coming, but he knew that he could not expect help from Italy, now openly pro-German, or from France, which had not even tried to stop Hitler in the Rhineland. He knew that perhaps his only chance at saving Austrian independence was to visit Hitler to try to find a peaceful solution.

On February 12, 1938, Schuschnigg and his foreign minister, Guido Schmidt,

Benito Mussolini (far left) reviews strategy with Hitler and his generals. In 1937, Italy joined Germany and Japan to form the "Axis" powers.

traveled in secret to Berchtesgaden (Eagles' Nest), Hitler's Bavarian mountain retreat. They were met at the border by Papen, now Hitler's ambassador to Austria. Papen smilingly welcomed the visitors, informing them that Hitler was in a jovial mood. When they arrived, however, they found that Hitler instead was in a foul mood and—just as alarming—was waiting for them dressed in the brown tunic of a storm trooper with three of his top generals at his side.

Haus Wachenfeld Obersalzberg.

At Berchtesgaden (pictured), Hitler tried to force Chancellor Kurt von Schuschnigg to give up Austria's independence.

Schuschnigg Under Fire

Once Schuschnigg and Hitler were alone, the Austrian leader attempted to begin the conversation with pleasantries. Hitler cut him off abruptly. "We did not gather here to speak of the fine view or of the weather,"[62] he said. The Nazi leader then launched into a lengthy tirade, accusing Austria of betraying the destiny of the German people. He scarcely gave his visitor a chance to speak, shouting,

> The whole history of Austria is just one uninterrupted act of high treason. That was so in the past, and is no better today. This historical paradox must now reach its long-overdue end. And I can tell you here and now, Herr Schuschnigg, that I am absolutely determined to make an end of all this. The German Reich is one of the Great Powers, and nobody will raise his voice if it settles its border problems.[63]

Finally, he told Schuschnigg, "Think it over well. I can only wait until this afternoon."[64] When the thoroughly cowed Schuschnigg asked what Hitler's terms were, he was told that could wait until after lunch.

After the meal, during which Hitler laughed and joked as if no disagreement had taken place, Schuschnigg was presented with a list of Germany's demands: The Nazi Party was to be legalized in Austria, Nazi sympathizer Artur Seyss-Inquart was to be made minister of the interior and thus in charge of the police, all Nazis in prison were to be freed and restored to their former jobs, a program of exchanging military officers was to be instituted, and work would begin on merging the two economies.

Schuschnigg realized he was looking at the death warrant of Austria. He attempted to negotiate some of the terms. Hitler told him, "You will either sign it as it is and fulfill my demands within three days, or I will order the march into Austria."[65] Schuschnigg protested. Even if he signed, he said, only the Austrian president could give final agreement.

Hitler flew into a rage. He flung open the door of his study, motioned Schuschnigg out, and shouted for one of his generals, Wilhelm Keitel, to come in. Sitting outside the study, Schuschnigg was terrified, thinking he had just doomed his country to invasion. Actually, it was pure bluff on Hitler's part. When Keitel asked for orders, Hitler grinned and said, "There are no orders. I just wanted you here."[66]

The Surrender

Thirty minutes passed before the Austrian chancellor was again ushered into the study. Hitler told him that, for the first time in his life, he had changed his mind—Austria would have six days instead of three to carry out the agreement. Now thoroughly demoralized, Schuschnigg signed.

Once back in Vienna, Schuschnigg presented the agreement to President Wilhelm Miklas. Miklas agreed to some of the provisions but refused to put Seyss-Inquart in charge of the police. Hitler, when he learned of this, ordered military mobilization on the Austrian border. Miklas gave in, and all provisions began to be implemented.

Schuschnigg had one final card to play. He called for a nationwide vote on March 13, 1938—yes or no to one statement: "We want a free and a German Austria, an independent and a social Austria, a Christian and a united Austria."[67] Hitler was furious. He had publicly maintained that a majority of Austrians wanted union with Germany. If the people of Austria voted otherwise, it would undercut his entire plan for annexation. He determined to prevent the election from taking place.

Early on the morning of March 11, Schuschnigg was awakened by the news that German troops were massed along the border. Seyss-Inquart, who was receiving his orders directly by telephone from Göring in Berlin, demanded that the election be canceled. Schuschnigg agreed. Then Göring increased the demands: Schuschnigg must resign and Seyss-Inquart be appointed chancellor. Some members of the Austrian cabinet thought this was too much and wanted to fight. Schuschnigg knew what the outcome would be and was determined to avoid needless bloodshed. He resigned, later saying,

Austria was a German state, and would be a German state when the confusing nightmare of National Socialism was long past, a historical memory of blood and tears. . . . My task was finished. I had done my duty to the best of my knowledge, and I refused to be instrumental—directly or indirectly—in the preparations for Cain once more to slay his brother Abel.[68]

Triumphal Return

Hitler, however, would not be robbed of a triumphal entry into the land of his birth. On Göring's orders, Seyss-Inquart "requested" the intervention of German troops to keep order. At dawn the next day, German tanks rolled across the Austrian border with Hitler in personal command. The convoy went through Linz, his boyhood home, and he stopped to make a speech:

When years ago I went forth from this town I bore within me precisely the same profession of faith which today fills my heart. Judge the depth of my emotion when after so many years I have been able to bring that profession of faith to its fulfillment. If Providence once called me forth from this town to be the leader of the Reich, it must in so doing have charged me with a mission, and that mission could only be to restore my dear homeland to the German Reich. I have believed in this mission, I have lived and fought for it, and I believe I have now fulfilled it.[69]

Two days later, Adolf Hitler returned as a conqueror to Vienna, the city in which he had once lived as a vagrant. He stayed only one night, but when he returned to Germany, Himmler stayed behind to launch a reign of SS terror. More than seventy thousand people were arrested, including Schuschnigg, who would remain in various concentration camps until the end of World War II. Hundreds of Jews were made to scrub the streets on their hands and knees while German soldiers stood by with rifles and Austrian citizens jeered.

On April 10, 1938, a national election was held, this time with Hitler's blessing. With most opposition either in concentration camps or frightened away, more than 99 percent of the voters approved becoming part of Germany. Austria ceased to exist; it now was Ostmark, a province of the Third Reich. According to Hitler, the medieval Holy Roman Empire had been the First Reich, or empire, and the unification of Germany under the Prussian kaisers in the late 1800s was the Second Reich.

Hitler was ecstatic. In only five years he had restored Germany's military might and brought about unification with Austria. He was by no means through. No sooner had he finished with Austria than he turned to his next target, Czechoslovakia, and took the next step toward plunging Europe and the rest of the world into war.

★ Chapter 6 ★

The Road to War: Czechoslovakia and Poland

By early 1938, Adolf Hitler had achieved a good part of his plan for the domination of Europe. Germany was again a major military power. Austria had been swallowed up by the Third Reich. Italy was an ally. Britain, France, and the Soviet Union were divided, hesitant, and confused. Hitler's next objective was to secure his southern front by dismembering Czechoslovakia. He would then be free to push eastward to Poland and beyond in his search for *Lebensraum* for the German people.

With Austria part of Germany, most of Czechoslovakia was now surrounded on three sides by the Nazi state. Czechoslovakia had been created by the peace treaties following World War I and incorporated many provinces of the old Austrian Empire. It was an economically strong, progressive democracy, but its weakness was that it comprised a host of ethnic groups, all of whom yearned for independence. About half the

---

After the occupation of Austria in 1938, Germany surrounded Czechoslovakia on three sides.

population was Czech, and Czechs held most of the top government posts. However, there were sizable numbers of Slovaks, Hungarians, Ruthenians, and—most important to Hitler's plans—about 3 million ethnic Germans living in an area known as the Sudetenland.

In 1933, a former gymnastics teacher named Konrad Henlein formed the Sudeten German Party. Within two years, the party was being funded by the Nazis and Henlein was taking orders directly from Berlin. Two weeks after the annexation of Austria, Hitler summoned Henlein and told him to make increasing demands on the Czech government. It was not that Hitler wanted any of the demands to be met. Far from it. As Henlein later said, "We must always demand so much that we can never be satisfied."[70]

Hitler wanted to use Nazis inside Czechoslovakia to create such a state of tumult that he would be "forced" to intervene to protect ethnic Germans. A year earlier, he had ordered his generals to draw up a plan, called Case Green, for an invasion. On May 20, 1938, he signed an updated Case Green, the first sentence of which read, "It is not my intention to smash Czechoslovakia by military action in the immediate future without provocation, unless an unavoidable development . . . *within* Czechoslovakia forces the issue."[71]

Hitler Backs Down

Word of German preparations for an invasion somehow reached the Czech government, but the Czechs expected the Germans to be on the march within days. Czech president Edvard Benes mobilized part of his forces on the German border and notified his French allies. Both France and Britain warned the Germans that an invasion would mean a European war.

The German army was, in fact, not sufficiently prepared to invade Czechoslovakia, which had a well-trained army and stout border defenses. In addition, Hitler would have had to leave his western border vulnerable should France elect to support Czechoslovakia. The Nazi dictator was furious, but backed down. On May 23 he had the German foreign office tell the Czechs, British, and French that he had no aggressive intentions toward Czechoslovakia.

This "May Crisis" had two long-term consequences. First, the humiliated Hitler developed a deep, savage hatred for Benes and the Czechs. He now told his generals, "It is my unalterable decision to smash Czechoslovakia by military action in the near future."[72] October 1, 1938, was set as the date for invasion. Second, even though the Germans had been warned by Britain and France, Hitler could see that Britain's support was, at best, unenthusiastic. While the French promised military support of Czechoslovakia, British diplomat Lord Halifax would say only that "it was impossible to foresee whether Britain would not be drawn into [a war]."[73]

Hitler's eagerness to fight a war for which Germany was not ready disturbed the most senior generals, particularly Chief of Staff Ludwig Beck. With amazing foresight, Beck predicted that Germany would have to fight Britain, France, and the Soviet Union, all supported—with matériel if not actual soldiers—by the United States. He failed to get the support of his fellow generals and resigned on August 19. His deputy, Franz Halder, replaced him. Unknown to Hitler, however, Halder shared Beck's view.

Believing that Germany would have to fight Britain, France, and the Soviet Union, Deputy Chief of Staff Franz Halder became part of a plot to overthrow Hitler.

Halder and Beck became the central figures in a plot to overthrow Hitler. They were joined by a small group of senior generals and others, many of whom had been ardent supporters of Hitler but were now disillusioned. The conspirators planned to wait until Hitler issued an order for an invasion of Czechoslovakia, then arrest him and put him on trial on the charge that he was not competent to govern.

The British Stance

The conspirators would argue that to invade Czechoslovakia would have led both France and Britain to attack Germany in the west. They were fairly certain that France would honor its alliance with Czechoslovakia, but would Britain?

To try to measure Britain's willingness to fight, the conspirators sent agents to London to warn the British of Hitler's invasion plans. British prime minister Neville Chamberlain, writing to Foreign Secretary Lord Halifax, said that while not believing much of what the German agents were saying, "I don't feel sure that we ought not to do something."[74] On August 28, he instructed Britain's ambassador to Germany, Sir Neville Henderson, to arrange a personal meeting between himself and Hitler.

On September 12, Hitler was to deliver a major speech at the close of the annual Nazi Party rally. Many thought he would declare war on Czechoslovakia. As a huge crowd shouted approval, the Nazi leader lashed out at Beneš and the Czechs but stopped short of declaring war, saying only that there would be serious consequences if the Sudeten Germans did not receive what he called "justice."[75]

Meanwhile, the French government, deeply divided on the Czech question, turned to Chamberlain for help. The British prime minister telegraphed Hitler, offering to fly to Germany "to see you with a view to trying to find a peaceful solution."[76] Hitler accepted, and the two leaders met on September 15 at Berchtesgaden.

Hitler began with a long harangue about the supposed wrongs done to the Sudeten Germans by the Czechs and his determination to see justice done. Shouting, gesturing, hardly letting Chamberlain respond, he said he was willing to risk a world war rather than let the Czech situation linger. Suddenly, Chamberlain grew angry. "If the Führer is determined to settle this matter by force without waiting even for a discussion between ourselves to take place, what did he let me come here for?" he demanded. "I have wasted my time."[77]

Misplaced Trust

Hitler quickly changed his demeanor. Perhaps, he said, a peaceful solution could be found. Would Britain be willing to support a secession of the Sudetenland to Germany if the Sudeten Germans approved it in an election? Chamberlain told Hitler that he agreed in principle but would need the approval of his cabinet. Chamberlain de-

British prime minister Neville Chamberlain meets with Hitler at Berchtesgaden. Chamberlain hoped that the two could find a peaceful solution to the Czech situation.

parted for London, where he told a friend, "I got the impression that here was a man who could be relied upon when he had given his word."[78]

As Hitler prepared for the invasion, the British and French met to decide Czechoslovakia's fate without bothering to consult the Czechs. Their proposal to Hitler was that all areas in which the population was more than 50 percent German were to be turned over to Germany. In return, Britain and France were to guarantee the safety of what remained of Czechoslovakia.

Chamberlain returned to Germany on September 22, confident he had prevented war. But when he outlined the Anglo-French proposal, Hitler calmly replied, "I am exceedingly sorry, but after the events of the last few days this solution is no longer any use."[79] It was not enough for the territories to be turned over to Germany, he told the astounded prime minister, they must be occupied by German troops by October 10. When Chamberlain protested, Hitler "allowed" himself to revert to the original October 1 date.

Once back in London, Chamberlain was unable to get his cabinet to accept the latest proposals. The Czechs began to prepare for an invasion. France reluctantly promised to aid Czechoslovakia, and Chamberlain, even more reluctantly, promised to aid France.

Meanwhile, Hitler was having troubles of his own. His generals were pleading with him not to attack. Mussolini was showing reluctance to stand by Germany. Hitler began to have second thoughts. Late on the night of September 27, he telegraphed Chamberlain, leaving the door open for another meeting. Chamberlain proposed a meeting at which representatives of Germany, Britain, France, and Italy—but not Czechoslovakia—would meet in Munich to settle Czechoslovakia's fate.

The Munich Conference

Mussolini opened the Munich Conference on September 29, 1938, by presenting what he called his own plan. Actually, it had been written by the German foreign office the day before and differed little from Hitler's last proposal to Chamberlain. The date for occupation was changed to October 10, and an international commission was to draw the new borders. After some discussion, the British and French agreed to the "Italian" proposal.

It was up to the British and French to inform two Czech diplomats, who had been kept in an adjoining room, of their country's fate. They were told of the terms and shown a map of the territories they were to give up. When they protested, a British diplomat told them, "If you do not accept, you will have to settle your affairs with the Germans absolutely alone."[80]

The Munich Conference spelled the end not only of Czechoslovakia, but also of the plot to overthrow Hitler. Beck, Halder, and the rest had been prepared to place Hitler under arrest, but Chamberlain's last-minute intervention wrecked their plans. After World War II, Halder said, "We were

Chamberlain returns to London after his first meeting with Hitler. He holds the proposal stating that Britain would support the secession of the Sudetenland to Germany.

firmly convinced that we would be successful. But now came Mr. Chamberlain and with one stroke the danger of war was avoided."[81]

Although it appeared Hitler had received everything he wanted, he was privately disappointed that he would not ride into Prague, the Czech capital, as a conqueror the way he had done in Austria. But his triumphal entry was not canceled, only postponed. German troops quickly occupied the Sudetenland, the promised election was never held, and the German-dominated commission drew up the borders to give Hitler every possible military advantage.

Hitler would not rest, however, until Benes and the Czechs had been completely humiliated. On February 12, 1939, he demanded that leaders of the Slovak minority declare their independence from Czechoslovakia. If they did, he promised, he would "protect" them. If they did not, they would be invaded.

Britain Backs Away

When the Slovaks declared their independence on March 14, Chamberlain used it

Hitler and Hácha

The treatment accorded Austrian chancellor Kurt von Schuschnigg prior to Germany's takeover was repeated early in 1939 when Hitler planned to grab what had been left of Czechoslovakia after the Munich Agreement. Like Schuschnigg before him, the Czech president, Dr. Emil Hácha, tried a last-minute trip to Hitler on March 14, 1939, to try to save his country.

Hácha tried to convince Hitler to leave Czechoslovakia independent. Hitler would have none of it. He ranted and raved. As the night wore on, he told Hácha bluntly that German troops would invade Czechoslovakia at dawn the next morning—one way or another. If the Czechs resisted, he said, their army would be crushed. Only Hácha could prevent this bloodshed by agreeing to admit the Germans peacefully. At 2:15 A.M. Hitler dismissed Hácha, who then was bullied by Göring and Ribbentrop. A French diplomat, who later heard what happened from a reliable source, described the scene, as related in William L. Shirer's *The Rise and Fall of the Third Reich:*

The German ministers [Göring and Ribbentrop] were pitiless. They literally hunted Dr. Hácha and M. Chvalkovsky [the Czech foreign minister] around the table on which the documents were lying, thrusting them continually before them, pushing pens into their hands, incessantly repeating that if they continued in their refusal, half of Prague [the Czech capital] would lie in ruins from bombing within two hours.

At this point, Hácha slumped to the floor, having suffered a heart attack. Dr. Theodor Morrell, Hitler's personal physician, was called and administered an injection. Hácha revived sufficiently to talk into the telephone Ribbentrop thrust into his hand. He told his government in Prague to surrender. Then, after a second injection, he was able to regain his feet long enough to go back into Hitler's study to sign away his country's freedom.

The document was signed at 3:55 A.M. Two hours later, German troops crossed the border. The triumphant Hitler spent that night in the presidential palace in Prague.

as an excuse to back away from having to defend Czechoslovakia. He claimed that "the effect of this declaration put an end by internal disruption to the State whose frontier we had proposed to guarantee."[82] The next day, Hitler entered Prague, spending the night at the presidential palace formerly occupied by Benes.

Britain and France protested, but feebly. Nevertheless, they had learned two lessons. First, Hitler was not to be trusted. Second, he would not, as promised, be satisfied with assimilating all Germans into the Third Reich. By swallowing Czechoslovakia he demonstrated that no part of Europe was safe. And it was no secret what his next goal was. Already conditions were worsening between Germany and Poland.

Hitler actually regarded Poland more as a possible ally than an eventual foe. His eventual target, he knew, would be the Soviet Union, and the Poles were violently anti-Russian and anti-Communist. Furthermore, they had a long history of anti-Semitism and would likely agree with the Nazi view of the Jews. Once more, however, Hitler's vanity and territorial ambitions got in the way.

On October 24, 1938, less than a month after the Munich Conference, German Foreign Minister Joachim von Ribbentrop had met with Josef Lipski, the Polish ambassador, and told him the time had come to speak about the return of Danzig to Germany. This Baltic port had been made an international city, controlled by the League of Nations, after World War I. Two formerly German provinces had been given to Poland to form the "Polish Corridor," linking Danzig with Poland. The Polish Corridor separated East Prussia from the rest of Germany.

A month later, Ribbentrop received a reply from Jozef Beck, the Polish foreign minister. It was not what Hitler wanted to hear: "Any attempt to incorporate the Free City [Danzig] into the Reich, must inevitably lead to conflict."[83] Like Benes before him, Beck had angered Hitler, who responded by

Polish foreign minister Jozef Beck refused to return the port of Danzig to Germany. This action would ultimately lead to the invasion of Poland.

ordering his generals to prepare a plan to seize Danzig by force.

On January 5, 1939, Hitler met Beck at Berchtesgaden. Although he did not treat his guest as rudely as Austria's Schuschnigg, he made his demands clear: Germany wanted to take over Danzig and build a highway and railroad line from Germany to that port city. Beck, not wishing to anger Hitler, replied only that "the Danzig problem was a very difficult one."[84]

Poland Surrounded

The question became even more difficult when, in mid-March, Germany occupied what had been left of Czechoslovakia. Poland was now surrounded on three sides by German territory. In Berlin, Ribbentrop's attitude grew increasingly unfriendly. He restated Hitler's demands to the Polish ambassador and added that an answer should come quickly "lest the Chancellor [Hitler] should come to the conclusion that Poland was rejecting all his offers."[85] On March 26, Beck did just that.

Beck knew that his only chance of resisting Germany lay in alliances with Britain and France. He appealed to Britain and Chamberlain, who had at last awakened to the threat posed by Hitler, and had reacted with unaccustomed strength. He announced in Parliament on March 31 that Britain would unconditionally guarantee the independence of Poland.

A Czech woman weeps as she salutes German troops occupying what was left of her country.

Hitler, when he learned of the British stance, flew into a rage, shouting, "I'll cook them a stew that they'll choke on."[86] On April 3, he ordered his generals to draw up Case White, a plan for the invasion of Poland. The target date was September 1, 1939.

The generals were appalled. Poland presented no great problem, but a German takeover there would invite an attack by the Soviet Union. To fight England and France in the west and the Soviet Union in the east at the same time, the generals thought, was impossible. Hitler had already considered this situation and had a plan.

As far back as November 1938, Germany had acted to improve trade relations with the Soviet Union. The Soviet dictator, Josef Stalin, was deeply suspicious of Britain and France and suspected they might be pushing him into a war with Germany. In a speech on March 10, 1939, he said he was determined "not to let our country be drawn into conflict by warmongers, whose custom it is to let others pull their chestnuts out of the fire."[87] Another signal came on May 3 when the Soviet foreign minister, Maxim Litvinov, who favored a strong alliance with Britain and France, was replaced by Vyacheslav Molotov.

"No Conflicts"

Two weeks later, a high-ranking Soviet diplomat told his German counterpart that "there were no conflicts in foreign policy between Germany and the Soviet Union and that therefore there was no reason for any enmity between the two countries."[88] Shortly afterward, Berlin responded, instructing its ambassador in Moscow to tell Molotov that "the time has come to consider a pacification and normalization of German-Soviet Russian foreign relations."[89]

Molotov was a realist. He was neither pro-British nor pro-German. He wanted only the best alliance for the Soviet Union and was willing to play one side against the other. Accordingly, in early June, he suggested that the British send their foreign minister to Moscow. Lord Halifax, however, protested that "it was really impossible to get away."[90] Eventually, a low-level diplomat, William Strang, was sent to Moscow. Stalin and Molotov could not be blamed for thinking the British were not serious about an alliance.

Finally, in July, the British agreed to military-staff talks with the Soviet Union. The officers they sent, however, did not have powers to negotiate. Furthermore, they went to Russia by ship, a week's journey, instead of by air.

While the British dallied, the Germans did not. On August 3, Ribbentrop met with Georgi Astakhov, a Soviet diplomat, and later reported,

> I expressed the *German* wish for remolding German-Russian relations and stated that from the Baltic to the Black Sea there was no problem which could not be solved to our mutual satisfaction. In response to Astakhov's desire for more concrete conversations on topical questions . . . I declared myself ready for such conversations . . . [and] dropped a gentle hint at our coming to an understanding with Russia on the fate of Poland.[91]

In other words, Germany was signaling that it might be willing to divide Poland with the Soviets.

By now, Hitler had already decided that he would eventually invade Poland. As far back as May 23, 1939, he told his generals, "Further successes can no longer be attained without the shedding of blood. . . . Danzig is not the subject of dispute at all. It is a question of expanding our living space in the East."[92] And when the Italian foreign minister, Count Ciano, visited Ribbentrop on August 11, trying to avert or at least delay a conflict, he asked what Germany wanted—the Polish Corridor? Danzig? "Not that anymore," Ribbentrop replied. "We want war!"[93]

The Nonaggression Pact

The next day, a telegram arrived from Moscow. As Ciano watched, Hitler and Ribbentrop read it carefully. Hitler then turned to his visitor and said, "The Russians have agreed to a German political negotiator being sent to Moscow."[94]

Stalin, however, was in no great hurry. A trade agreement, he said, would need to be reached before any military matters could be taken up. The Soviet dictator still was playing the Germans and the western democracies against one another, but while Hitler seemed eager, even frantic, to conclude an alliance, the British and French were lukewarm. Three years later, Stalin said,

We formed the impression that the British and French Governments were not resolved to go to war if Poland were attacked, but that they hoped the diplomatic line-up of Britain, France and Russia would deter Hitler. We were sure it would not.[95]

Accordingly, the Soviets agreed that Ribbentrop would come to Moscow with full powers to negotiate a military nonaggression treaty. The German foreign minister arrived at the Kremlin on August 23, 1939, and the agreement was signed that night. In addition to what was publicly announced— a pledge not to attack one another for at least ten years—the treaty contained a secret clause dividing Poland between the two countries and giving the Russians a free hand in Finland, Estonia, Latvia, and Lithuania.

Soviet foreign minister Vyacheslav Molotov (seated) signs the nonaggression pact with Germany while Ribbentrop (third from right) and Stalin (second from right) observe.

It was now only a matter of time before the outbreak of war. Hitler wanted to launch an attack on August 25, but delayed at the last moment for two reasons. First, Mussolini continued to protest that Italy was not ready for war. Second, and more important to Hitler, Britain and Poland signed a mutual-assistance agreement. He recovered his confidence, however, and the attack was scheduled for September 1.

In Rome, the pope made an appeal for peace. So did President Roosevelt. The British and French made final pleas to Hitler even as they warned him they would support Poland. The French premier, Edouard Daladier, wrote

If the blood of France and of Germany flows again, as it did twenty-five years ago, in a longer and even more murderous war, each of the two peoples will fight with confidence in its own victory, but the most certain victors will be the forces of destruction and barbarism.[96]

Hitler could not be swayed. He believed his hour, the hour of German destiny, had come. On August 31, SS men dressed in Polish army uniforms seized a radio station just inside Germany, fired a

President Franklin Delano Roosevelt made an appeal for a peaceful solution to the Polish crisis. His efforts, as well as those of Britain and France, were in vain.

few shots, broadcast an anti-German speech in Polish, and departed. Behind them, to help make it look even more like a Polish attack, they left the bodies of some concentration camp prisoners who had been dressed in Polish uniforms and then shot.

The Reply to Roosevelt

As tension between Germany and Poland mounted in 1939, U.S. president Franklin Roosevelt telegraphed Hitler and Italian dictator Benito Mussolini to try to get from them a promise to respect the sovereignty of other nations. Roosevelt's wording, taken from Shirer's *The Rise and Fall of the Third Reich*, was blunt: "Are you willing to give assurance that your armed forces will not attack or invade the territory of the following independent nations?" This was followed by a list of thirty nations. On April 28, Hitler replied in a speech to the Reichstag. After heaping scorn on the United States for its failure to join the League of Nations and for its treatment of the Native American population, he answered Roosevelt's question:

> How has Mr. Roosevelt learned which nations consider themselves threatened by German policy and which do not? Or is Mr. Roosevelt

in a position, in spite of the enormous amount of work which must rest upon him in his own country, to recognize of his own accord all these inner spiritual and mental impressions of other people and their governments? Finally, Mr. Roosevelt asks that assurance be given him that the German armed forces will not attack, and above all, not invade the territory or possessions of the following independent nations. . . .

He then read the list of nations very slowly, ranging from the great powers such as Great Britain and France to the tiny principalities of Luxembourg and Monaco. As he read, the Reichstag deputies began to chuckle, then to laugh, then to roar. In the tumult, no one seemed to note that Hitler had omitted one nation—Poland—from the list. Four months later, Germany invaded Poland, igniting World War II.

On this pretext, German troops poured across the Polish border on the morning of September 1, 1939. Tanks raced through fields and villages, and dive bombers rained destruction on cities in a new form of combat known as *Blitzkrieg*, or lightning war. After some hesitation, Britain and France declared war on Germany on September 3. World War II had begun.

Chapter 7

The Third Reich at War

Adolf Hitler's approach to war reflected his own personality—mercurial, impulsive, given to sudden bursts of wild energy. His strategy for winning World War II was a series of quick, massive blows. Unfortunately for Germany, their leader had dragged the country into a long, drawn-out conflict for which it was not prepared psychologically, militarily, or financially. So strong was Hitler's hold over the German people, however, that the vast majority stayed loyal and obedient even as their country was being destroyed.

Despite the barrage of war fever propaganda from Goebbels, most Germans thought war would be averted at the last minute. After all, hadn't their Führer taken Austria and Czechoslovakia without a response from the spineless British and French? Consequently, they were dazed on September 3, 1939, when loudspeakers announced that their country was at war with both western democracies. Journalist William Shirer witnessed the scene:

Some 250 people were standing there in the sun. They listened attentively to the announcement. When it was finished, there was

German troops invade Poland. Britain and France responded to this attack by declaring war on Germany.

not a murmur. They just stood there as they were before. Stunned. The people cannot realize yet that Hitler has led them into a world war.[97]

Shirer compared the mood of the Germans in 1939 to what he observed on the day World War I began: "In 1914, I believe, the excitement in Berlin on the first day of the

World War was tremendous. Today, no excitement, no hurrahs, no cheering, no throwing of flowers, no war fever, no war hysteria."[98]

Even the Nazi leaders seemed overwhelmed by events. When the British war ultimatum was read to him, Hitler sat motionless for a few moments as the rest of the room froze in silence. Finally, he turned slowly to Ribbentrop and growled, "What now?" In the next room, Göring, for once not full of bluff and bluster, said, "If we lose this war, then God help us!"[99]

The Fall of France

From the outbreak of the war to 1942, however, there seemed to be little chance of Germany's losing the war. Hitler's troops quickly overran Poland while Britain and France sat idle in the west. Then, in May 1940, Hitler ended the *Sitzkrieg*, or "sitting war" as the Germans nicknamed it, by sweeping through Belgium and the Netherlands into France. In only five weeks' fighting, the proud French were beaten. Hitler further humiliated them by accepting their surrender near the town of Compiègne in the same railroad car in which the Germans had signed the armistice ending World War I.

Hitler's popularity in Germany was at an all-time high. Everywhere he went he was met by adoring crowds. Women and children reached out to touch him, crying, "*Heil*, Hitler!" The group that had plotted to arrest him was still meeting, convinced his success could not last. While it did, however, they could only bide their time.

Hitler's Finest Hour

It took only four weeks for the Germans' *Blitzkrieg* to conquer France, thereby wiping out the humiliation of their defeat in World War I. Hitler personally accepted the surrender of the French at Compiègne, France, in the same railroad car in which Germany had signed the armistice on November 11, 1918.

On June 21, 1940, Hitler, accompanied by Göring, Ribbentrop, and a host of generals, arrived at the scene, described by William L. Shirer in his *Berlin Diary*:

> I observed his face. It was grave, solemn, yet brimming with revenge. There was also in it, as in his springy step, a note of the triumphant conqueror, the defier of the world. There was something else . . . a sort of scornful, inner joy at being present at this great reversal of fate—a reversal he himself had wrought.
>
> . . . He glances slowly around the clearing, and now, as his eyes meet ours, you grasp the depth of his hatred. But there is triumph there too—revengeful, triumphant hate. Suddenly, as though his face were not giving quite complete expression to his feelings, he throws his whole body into harmony with his mood. He swiftly snaps his hands on his hips, arches his shoulders, plants his feet wide apart. It is a magnificent gesture of defiance, of burning contempt for this place now and all that it has stood for in the twenty-two years since it witnessed the humbling of the German Empire.

Only Great Britain stood against Germany, and on August 13, 1940, Göring unleashed his air force against the island nation in a months-long bombing attack designed to force the British to sue for peace. The British Royal Air Force, fighting heroically against superior odds, battled the *Luftwaffe* to a standstill over the English Channel, and a scheduled invasion by the Germans was called off in November.

It was the night bombing of London, known as the blitz, that brought the war to Germany. On August 24, eighty-one British Lancaster bombers set out for Berlin on a retaliatory strike. Only about half reached their target, and the physical damage they inflicted was small. The psychological damage, however, was great. Back in 1939, Göring had boasted that his air force was so strong that if ever an enemy bomb fell on Germany "you can call me Meier [a Jewish name]!"[100] In his diary on August 26, Shirer recorded,

The Berliners are stunned. They did not think it could happen. When this war began, Göring assured them it couldn't. . . . The Berliners are a naïve and simple people. They believed him. Their disillusionment today therefore is all the greater. You have to see their faces to measure it. Göring made matters worse by informing the population only three days ago that they need not go to their cellars when the sirens sounded.[101]

The Air Raids

Not until 1942 would Germany suffer the same heavy bombings as London had two years earlier. On May 31 the British launched the first major raid, sending more than a thousand planes against a single city,

Cologne. The entire center of Cologne was consumed by the resulting firestorm, and the only structure left standing was the cathedral. Similar raids were carried out against other cities, including Hamburg, where a four-night raid destroyed 80 percent of the city and killed eighty thousand people.

In November, heavy raids began to pound Berlin. From then until the end of the war, day after day, American planes would attack by day and the British by night, led to their target by the fires caused by the American bombs. By war's end, virtually the entire city had been destroyed.

The most devastating air raid against Germany, however, was to take place on February 14, 1945. Allied aircraft poured tons of incendiary bombs, those designed to cause fires rather than explosions, on Dresden. So intense was the inferno created in the city's center that it consumed all the oxygen in the air and sucked air in from the edges, feeding the flames even more. The city was crowded with refugees, and more than one hundred thousand died, most of them not from explosions or falling debris, but in their air raid shelters from suffocation. The death toll in Dresden would be exceeded only by the atomic bomb raids on the Japanese cities of Hiroshima and Nagasaki later that year.

Even amid the destruction, the Germans stayed loyal to Hitler. Near the end, when virtually all military men knew the war was lost, Albert Speer, Hitler's architect and minister of munitions, spoke with some

farmers who changed his flat tire on a country road near Westphalia. As Speer later related,

Dresden lies in ruins after the Allied incendiary raid on February 14, 1945. More than one hundred thousand people died in the firestorm.

> To my surprise, the faith in Hitler which had been hammered into their minds all these last years was still strong. Hitler could never lose the war, they declared! The Führer is still holding something in reserve that he'll play at the last moment. Then the turning point will come. It's only a trap, his letting the enemy come so far into our country![102]

The Attack on Russia

The destruction of Germany was still far in the future, however, when Hitler made the decision that would change the course of World War II. On June 22, 1941, he launched Operation Barbarossa, a massive surprise attack on the Soviet Union. The Soviets, unprepared, fell back as German armies pushed east. Behind the German

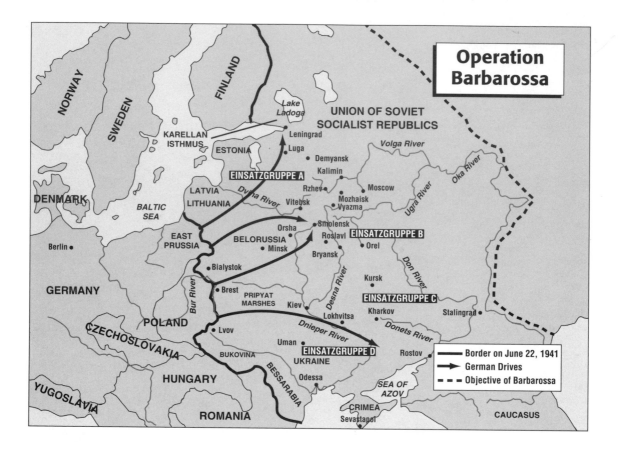

armies came the *Einsatzgruppen*, whose mission was to find and exterminate as many Communist officials and Jews and Gypsies as possible. Their method of operation was to surround a town or village, usually just before dawn, gather their victims, and march them to a remote location where they mowed them down with machine guns and buried the bodies in huge pits. At Babi Yar, on the outskirts of Kiev in the western Soviet Union at least 50,000 Ukrainians, of whom 33,000 were Jews, were killed on a single day. By September 1941 an estimated 700,000 Jews had been killed.

Such a death count was not nearly enough for Hitler. His goal was nothing less than the extermination of every Jew in Europe. This program, called by the Nazis "the Final Solution to the Jewish question," became known to later generations as the Holocaust.

Eventually, six death camps—Auschwitz-Birkenau, Sobibor, Treblinka, Majdanek, Chelmno, and Belzec—were established in Poland. When the mass gassings finally ended at Auschwitz-Birkenau in January 1945, an estimated 6 million Jews had been slaughtered.

The Nazis had taken great pains to hide what they were doing, but nothing undertaken on so massive a scale could be kept a secret. Death camp guards, home on leave, told relatives and friends —either in hushed whispers or drunken boasts—what was happening. Within Germany, the civilian population could not help but know what was taking place, especially when the wind brought the stench of death from nearby concentration camps.

Despite the years of Nazi propaganda to which they had been subjected, millions of ordinary Germans both in and out of uniform were deeply disturbed. They no longer believed as much in what they were fighting for. One German general admitted after the war, "The Allied cause was better than ours. The transgressions of Hitler had created a moral vacuum in the German forces." [103]

The Greatest Blunder?

The invasion of the Soviet Union has been called Hitler's greatest blunder, but it is difficult, considering the man and his lifelong philosophy, to see what else he would have done. The archenemies of the *Volk*, according to Hitler, were the Jews and the Communists. If Germany was to achieve its *Lebensraum*, it could be done only at the expense of the Soviet Union. Also, Hitler wanted to be the one to strike first. Late in the war he said,

Victims of a death camp are piled onto a cart for disposal. An estimated 6 million Jews and countless others were executed by the Nazis.

My own personal nightmare was the fear that Stalin might take the initiative before me. . . . If I felt compelled to settle my accounts with Bolshevism by force of arms . . . I have every right to believe that Stalin had come to the same decision even before he signed the pact [of 1939]. War with Russia had become inevitable, whatever we did and to postpone it only meant that we should later have to fight it under conditions far less favourable.[104]

Hitler's other major blunder was to declare war on the United States immediately after Japan's sneak attack on the U.S. naval base at Pearl Harbor on December 7, 1941. Germany was under no obligation to do so, even though the two nations were allies. Japan, in fact, had signed a nonaggression treaty with the Soviet Union rather than attack the Soviets from the east when the Germans attacked from the west.

Several theories have been suggested as to why Hitler declared war on the United States, but two seem most likely. First, President Roosevelt had greatly angered Hitler by sending him warnings during the Czech and Polish crises and thus "meddling" in European affairs. Roosevelt had also furnished considerable material aid to the British, despite the supposed neutrality of the United States.

Second, Hitler completely underestimated both the economic and military capacity of the Americans. He considered the United States a "mongrel" nation of mixed races and nationalities, dominated by Jews, and failed to foresee either the ability of its industry to mobilize or the ability of its people to fight.

November 1942 was the turning point of the war in Europe. On the 5th, Germany's Africa Corps, under the command of General Erwin Rommel, was defeated by the British at El Alamein, Egypt, thus blocking the German advance toward the vital Suez Canal. On the 11th, American troops under General Dwight Eisenhower landed far to the west in Morocco. Caught between the Allies, the Germans would eventually retreat from North Africa, leaving Italy open to invasion.

Stalingrad

The other key battle of November 1942 took place in the Soviet Union. Ever since July, the Germans had been trying to capture the city of Stalingrad. They eventually did, but the German supply lines were dangerously extended and the troops faced a bitter winter. On November 19, the Soviets attacked from the Germans' northern and southern flanks and succeeded in encircling the German Sixth Army west of Stalingrad. Despite Hitler's frantic orders to fight until the last soldier was dead, General Friedrich von Paulus surrendered his remaining troops. Only five thousand eventually returned to Germany. Two months later, the Soviets recaptured Stalingrad and began the offensive that would eventually lead them to Berlin.

Two British soldiers capture a German tank crewman at El Alamein. Germany's defeat in North Africa was the turning point of the war in Europe.

From 1939 to 1942 it had appeared as if nothing could halt the German army. It swept through Poland, Norway, Belgium, the Netherlands, France, and much of the Soviet Union like a well-oiled machine. As the war dragged on, however, the flaws in the machine began to show. Germany's military leadership was badly uncoordinated as top generals vied with one another and with Nazi leaders for power. On December 16, 1941, Hitler, who never trusted the generals, assumed personal overall command. Consequently, commanders in the field were stripped of their ability to exploit sudden advantages by taking independent action. Every major decision had to be bucked up the line until it finally arrived on Hitler's desk. His unstable personality only added to the confusion. Historian Alan Clark called the German military "a lumpish hexagonal pyramid with Hitler at its summit."[105]

In addition to an inefficient command structure, the German war machine suffered from a lack of resources. As many of the generals had realized, Germany lacked the natural resources for a prolonged war. The country had to depend heavily on imports for raw materials—45 percent of its iron ore, 50 percent of its lead, 70 percent of its copper. For some metals, such as chromium and tungsten, Germany had to depend entirely on imports.

Failure of the Economy

The lack of raw materials was compounded by Hitler's failure to order the entire German economy mobilized for war. The general in charge of armaments, Georg Thoma, saw the problem and urged Hitler to arm Germany "in depth," rapidly expanding heavy industry to produce the weapons needed for a long war. Such a policy, however, would have caused a shortage of consumer goods, and Hitler, wanting to ensure his popularity and keep civilian morale high, elected to produce only enough armaments to fuel his *Blitzkrieg* strategy.

For the early years of the war, Hitler's industrial strategy seemed to work. The army won victory after victory, and tons of consumer goods from the conquered countries flooded into Germany. After 1941, however, there were no more cheap victories, and the flow of captured goods slowed to a trickle. Hitler finally saw his error early in 1942 and ordered war production stepped up, but it was too late.

By mid-1942, Nazi Germany had reached the zenith of its power, stretching from the southern border of France to just west of Moscow—a territory far too large for the German economy and military to sustain. El Alamein and Stalingrad were the beginning of the end. On September 3, 1943, Allied forces landed in Italy, and Hitler had to prop up Mussolini with troops badly needed elsewhere. On June 6, 1944, Americans, Britons, and Canadians swarmed onto the beaches of Normandy in France and began the long push into Germany.

As the Allies began to close in on Germany, Hitler's behavior grew even more unstable. It was almost as if he could keep defeat at a distance by refusing to look at the evidence of its approach. He refused to view the devastation caused by Allied bombing on his cities and would often travel by night to avoid doing so. Once when his train stopped on a track next to a train carrying wounded soldiers back from the Soviet front, he ordered the blinds drawn. If dispatches from his generals were too pessimistic, he threw them aside unread. He seldom appeared in public, preferring to stay in semi-seclusion, surrounded only by a few loyal aides and secretaries.

Hitler's Health

As Germany's military failed, so did Hitler's health. He developed a facial twitch, and his left arm and leg would sometimes tremble uncontrollably. General Heinz Guderian remembered that eventually

> It was no longer simply his left hand, but the whole left side of his body that trembled. . . . He walked awkwardly, stooped more than ever, and his gestures were both jerky and slow. He had to have a chair pushed beneath him when he wished to sit down.[106]

Part of Hitler's physical troubles may have been caused by the daily injections of a questionable combination of drugs administered by Dr. Theodor Morrell. Experts have concluded that by the war's end, Hitler was completely addicted to these drugs, which probably further unbalanced his mind.

As Germany's military fortunes diminished, the group conspiring to remove Hitler renewed their attempts. Hitler was close to being assassinated several times during 1943 and 1944, but luck always intervened. Once, a time bomb placed aboard a plane behind his seat failed to go off. On another occasion, a bomb timed to go off during a visit by Hitler to the Bürgerbräukeller beer hall in Munich exploded prematurely. A young officer volunteered for a suicide bombing during

Hitler's inspection of a uniform factory, but an Allied bomb destroyed the building the day before the tour and Hitler's visit was canceled.

The last and most serious attempt to kill Hitler came on July 20, 1944, when Colonel Claus von Stauffenberg, a much-wounded war hero, carried a briefcase containing a time bomb into a room where Hitler was conducting a military conference. He placed the briefcase on the floor, only a few feet from Hitler, then left the room unobserved. Another officer, trying to get a better view of a map, moved the briefcase to the far side of a heavy table support. When the bomb exploded, the main force of the explosion was directed away from Hitler. Although cut and bruised, he survived.

Hitler's Revenge

Stauffenberg did not survive. The SS arrested everyone remotely connected with the plot. Some, including Stauffenberg and General Ludwig Beck, were lined up against a wall and shot. Others were hanged so that they would slowly strangle to death instead of suffering broken necks. Their deaths were filmed so that Hitler could view them again and again.

Finally, when the Soviets were closing in on Berlin and the city was under heavy artillery fire, Hitler retreated to a concrete bunker fifty feet below his Chancellery, sleeping and waking at odd times as others tried to adapt to his schedule. In this strange world where there was neither night nor day, Hitler planned elaborate counterattacks using forces that existed only in his mind.

At last, even Hitler realized all was lost. He determined not to be taken alive. He dictated a long, rambling last testament, blaming everyone except himself for what had befallen Germany. Above all, he blamed "the universal poisoner of all peoples, international Jewry."[107] On April 30, 1945, he said farewell to those who had remained with him. He and Eva Braun, his longtime mistress whom he had married the day before, then went into their room and closed the door. Soon, a shot rang out.

Hitler visits one of the officers wounded in the July 20, 1944, assassination attempt. Hitler would eventually die by his own hand.

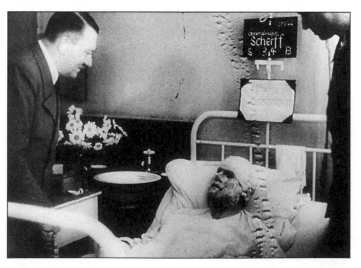

Hitler's Will

A few hours before he committed suicide in an underground bunker in April 1945, Adolf Hitler dictated a long final statement in which he claimed that he had been betrayed by the military and his closest advisers and lashed out once more at the Jews. Shortly afterward, he dictated a much shorter document, his last will and testament, quoted in Alan Bullock's *Hitler: A Study in Tyranny.*

Although I did not consider that I could take the responsibility during the years of struggle of contracting a marriage, I have now decided, before the end of my life, to take as my wife the woman [Eva Braun] who, after many years of faithful friendship, of her own free will entered this town [Berlin], when it was already besieged, in order to share my fate. At her own desire she goes to death with me as my wife. This will compensate us for what we have both lost through my work in the service of my people.

What I possess belongs—in so far as it has any value—to the Party, or, if this no longer exists, to the State. Should the State too be destroyed, no further decision on my part is necessary.

My pictures, in the collection which I have bought in the course of years, have never been collected for private purposes, but only for the establishment of a gallery in my home-town of Linz on the Danube.

It is my heartfelt wish that this bequest should be duly executed.

As my executor I nominate my most faithful Party comrade, Martin Bormann. He is given full legal authority to make all decisions. He is permitted to hand to my relatives anything which has a sentimental value or is necessary for the maintenance of a modest standard of life; especially for my wife's mother and my faithful fellow-workers who are well known to him. The chief of these are my former secretaries, Frau Winter, etc., who have for many years helped me by their work.

I myself and my wife choose to die in order to escape the disgrace of deposition or capitulation. It is our wish to be burned immediately in the place where I have carried out the greater part of my daily work in the course of my twelve years' service to my people.

After a few moments the others entered, finding the Nazi Führer lying on a sofa dead, shot through the mouth. Beside him was the body of Eva Braun, who had swallowed poison. The bodies were carried up into the Chancellery, placed in a shallow grave, doused with gasoline, and set ablaze. As the flames mounted, Goebbels and the others raised their arms in the Nazi salute.

The Third Reich did not long outlive its leader. A week later, on May 7, the man Hitler had named to succeed him, Admiral Karl Dönitz, signed an unconditional surrender at Reims, France. World War II was over in Europe. It would last a few more months in the Pacific until Japan, devastated by the nuclear destruction of Hiroshima and Nagasaki, also surrendered. Across the globe, 55 million people had lost their lives—in battle, in bombings, in prison, or in death camps. The Nazi Party was dead. Adolf Hitler was dead. Together, however, they had brought misery and death on a level without parallel in the history of humankind.

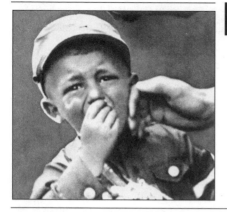

The Tragedy of "What If?"

World War II was, in very large measure, Adolf Hitler's war. While it can be argued that eventually Japan would have attempted expansion in the Pacific and the Soviet Union would have tried to take over eastern Europe, Hitler and the Nazis bear the blame for a program of aggression that plunged the world into bloody conflict. Who, however, bears the blame for Hitler and the Nazis?

The question of how an obscure corporal, so recently a penniless vagrant, could have risen to such heights and carried his nation to such depths has fascinated historians. They have pointed to the German heritage of obedience to authority, its lack of democratic traditions, the humiliating defeat of World War I and the Treaty of Versailles, the hardships of the Great Depression, the fear of communism, the history of German anti-Semitism, and the raw force of Hitler's personality. It was not any one, but rather a combination of all these factors that eventually spewed forth National Socialism.

Hitler made no secret of his entire political, racial, and military agenda, but rather set it out completely in *Mein Kampf.* Why then, when he was recognized as a menace at various times on his climb to dominance, was he not stopped? In blaming Hitler for World War II, one must also blame those who had opportunities to halt him and failed to do so.

Either the military or the business/industrial establishment could have ended Hitler's career at any time between 1920 and 1933. Both sectors looked upon the Nazi leader as crude and somewhat comical. Though not overly fond of Jews, they had little use for his racial rantings about subhumans and master races. In Hitler, however, both business and the military found someone who could weld the German people and restore the country to greatness. The generals and capitalists thought they could give him their support,

The Nuremberg Trials

Immediately after World War II, the highest-ranking captured Nazi leaders were put on trial at Nuremberg, ironically the site of the party's greatest rallies. The twenty-two defendants included Hermann Göring, Rudolf Hess, Joachim von Ribbentrop, Hans Frank (Hitler's attorney and governor-general of Poland), Julius Streicher, Albert Speer, Artur Seyss-Inquart, and Franz von Papen.

Some of the defendants, such as Göring, claimed to know nothing about the extermination of the Jews in the death camps. Others said they had no choice, that they were only following Hitler's orders. "Even with all this I know," said Ribbentrop, quoted in Louis Snyder's *Encyclopedia of the Third Reich*, "if in this cell Hitler should come to me and say, 'Do this!' I would still do it." Still others, like Streicher, were unrepentant, vowing they would do the same things if given another chance.

Shortly after 1 A.M. on October 16, 1946, Ribbentrop and nine of his fellow defendants were hanged in the Nuremberg prison. Göring, however, escaped the noose. Two hours before his scheduled execution, he swallowed poison that had been smuggled into his cell.

Only a very few of the defendants in the Nuremberg trials or any of the other war crimes trials seemed to be honestly sorry for the years of suffering and the millions of deaths they had caused. One was Frank, who confessed his crimes and added, as quoted in William L. Shirer's *The Rise and Fall of the Third Reich*, "A thousand years will pass and the guilt of Germany will not be erased."

Hermann Göring, Rudolf Hess, Joachim von Ribbentrop, and other captured Nazi leaders are seen here during their trial for war crimes at Nuremberg.

go along for the ride, then cast him aside when they wished. When the time came that they no longer needed Hitler, he had become far too powerful. Their opportunity to stop Nazism was lost in their own greed and self-interest.

The churches—both Roman Catholic and Lutheran—were the only German institutions with enough moral force to have turned the people away from the Nazis.

While many brave clergymen did indeed speak out, and thereby suffered arrest and imprisonment, the majority kept quiet, not heeding Pastor Martin Niemöller's declaration in 1937: "No more are we ready to keep silent at man's behest when God commands us to speak."[108] Also, the record of the Roman Catholic Church bureaucracy in Rome, especially the signing of an agreement with the Nazis in 1933, must be questioned.

Britain and France must also share the blame for Hitler's success. When Hitler sent troops into the Rhineland in 1935, Britain and France had the military might and legal right to act against him, but they lacked the will. Instead, they bent over backwards to avoid a conflict while the Nazis swallowed up Austria and Czechoslovakia. When the British and French finally, and still reluctantly, confronted Hitler over Poland, it was too late. By trying desperately to avoid a war, they found themselves enmeshed in one they almost lost.

Finally, what about the German people who voted for Hitler in ever-increasing numbers, who cheered madly at Nazi ral-

Like this young boy, many Germans were too frightened by Hitler to take any action against him.

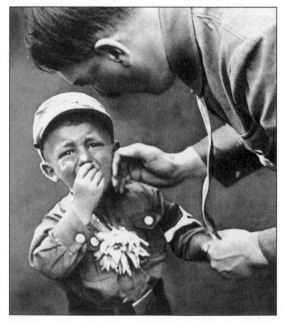

lies, whose freedoms and constitutional rights were stripped away, and who eventually died by the hundreds of thousands in bomb-torn cities? Despite the large crowds and all the "*Heil,* Hitlers," the ordinary Germans were never overly enthusiastic about the Nazis prior to 1933. Even two months after Hitler took power and the SA and Gestapo were rounding up his opponents and clapping them into concentration camps, the Nazis polled only 44 percent of the vote in Reichstag elections.

The ordinary Germans, however, were either too frightened, too apathetic, or too motivated by self-interest to take any action. William Shirer recalled conversations with Germans who opposed Hitler. "What could they do?" he wrote. "They would often put the question to you, and it was not an easy one to answer." [109]

In the end, no one—not business, the military, the church, other countries, or the German people—attempted to do anything until it was too late. It was as if none of them wanted to get involved in events, only to have events overtake them. As Pastor Niemöller wrote:

> First the Nazis went after the Jews, but I was not a Jew, so I did not object. Then they went after the Catholics, but I was not a Catholic, so I did not object. Then they went after the trade-unionists, but I was not a trade-unionist, so I did not object. Then they came after me, and there was no one left to object. [110]

★ Notes ★

Chapter One: The Young Hitler

1. Quoted in Alan Bullock, *Hitler: A Study in Tyranny*. New York: Harper & Row, 1962, p. 27.
2. Quoted in Bullock, *Hitler*, p. 27.
3. Quoted in William L. Shirer, *The Rise and Fall of the Third Reich*. New York: Simon & Schuster, 1960, p. 12.
4. Quoted in Shirer, *The Rise and Fall of the Third Reich*, p. 13.
5. Quoted in August Kubizek, *The Young Hitler I Knew*. Westport, CT: Greenwood Press, 1976, p. 55.
6. Kubizek, *The Young Hitler I Knew*, p. 55.
7. Kubizek, *The Young Hitler I Knew*, p. 96.
8. Kubizek, *The Young Hitler I Knew*, p. 100.
9. Kubizek, *The Young Hitler I Knew*, p. 153.
10. Quoted in Bullock, *Hitler*, p. 33.
11. Quoted in Shirer, *The Rise and Fall of the Third Reich*, p. 18.
12. Quoted in Klaus P. Fischer, *Nazi Germany: A New History*. New York: Continuum, 1995, p. 88.
13. Quoted in Shirer, *The Rise and Fall of the Third Reich*, p. 26.
14. Quoted in Kubizek, *The Young Hitler I Knew*, p. 79.
15. Quoted in Shirer, *The Rise and Fall of the Third Reich*, p. 26.
16. Quoted in Shirer, *The Rise and Fall of the Third Reich*, pp. 22–23.
17. Quoted in T. L. Jarman, *The Rise and Fall of Nazi Germany*. New York: New York University Press, 1956, p. 111.
18. Quoted in Bullock, *Hitler*, p. 48.
19. Quoted in Bullock, *Hitler*, p. 50.
20. Quoted in Bullock, *Hitler*, p. 53.
21. Quoted in Shirer, *The Rise and Fall of the Third Reich*, p. 38.

Chapter Two: The Road to Power

22. Quoted in Shirer, *The Rise and Fall of the Third Reich*, p. 40.
23. Quoted in Bullock, *Hitler*, p. 69.
24. Quoted in Bullock, *Hitler*, pp. 373–74.
25. Quoted in Fischer, *Nazi Germany*, p. 154.
26. Quoted in Fischer, *Nazi Germany*, pp. 161–62.
27. Quoted in Bullock, *Hitler*, p. 130.
28. Quoted in Shirer, *The Rise and Fall of the Third Reich*, p. 136.
29. Quoted in Fischer, *Nazi Germany*, p. 234.
30. Quoted in Otto Friedrich, *Before the Deluge: A Portrait of Berlin in the 1920's*. New York: Harper & Row, 1972, p. 381.
31. Quoted in Friedrich, *Before the Deluge*, p. 282.

Chapter Three: The Nazification of Germany

32. Quoted in Shirer, *The Rise and Fall of the Third Reich*, p. 201.
33. Quoted in Shirer, *The Rise and Fall of the Third Reich*, p. 217.
34. Quoted in Fischer, *Nazi Germany*, p. 355.
35. Quoted in Fischer, *Nazi Germany*, p. 355.
36. Quoted in Shirer, *The Rise and Fall of the Third Reich*, p. 249.
37. Quoted in Fischer, *Nazi Germany*, p. 359.
38. Quoted in Shirer, *The Rise and Fall of the Third Reich*, p. 244.
39. Quoted in Fischer, *Nazi Germany*, p. 368.

Chapter Four: The Fate of the Jews

40. Fischer, *Nazi Germany*, p. 390.
41. Quoted in John Weiss, *Ideology of Death: Why the Holocaust Happened in Germany*. Chicago: Ivan R. Dee, 1996, p. 23.
42. Quoted in Louis L. Snyder, *Encyclopedia of the Third Reich*. New York: Paragon House, 1989, p. 96.
43. Quoted in Fischer, *Nazi Germany*, p. 392.
44. Quoted in Shirer, *The Rise and Fall of the Third Reich*, p. 431.
45. Quoted in Shirer, *The Rise and Fall of the Third Reich*, p. 432.
46. Quoted in Fischer, *Nazi Germany*, p. 504.
47. Quoted in Rudolf Höss, Pery Broad, and Johann Paul Kremer, *KL Auschwitz Seen by the SS*. Edited by Jadwiga Bezwinska and Danuta Czech. Translated by Constantine Fitzgibbon, Krystyna Michalik, and Zbignew Bezwinski. New York: Howard Fertig, 1984, p. 109.

Chapter Five: The Road to War: Weakness to Strength

48. Quoted in Jarman, *The Rise and Fall of Nazi Germany*, p. 206.
49. Quoted in Fischer, *Nazi Germany*, p. 403.
50. Quoted in Jarman, *The Rise and Fall of Nazi Germany*, p. 210.
51. Quoted in Jarman, *The Rise and Fall of Nazi Germany*, p. 210.
52. Quoted in Fischer, *Nazi Germany*, p. 405.
53. Quoted in Shirer, *The Rise and Fall of the Third Reich*, p. 280.
54. Quoted in Jarman, *The Rise and Fall of Nazi Germany*, p. 213.
55. Quoted in Jarman, *The Rise and Fall of Nazi Germany*, p. 215.
56. William L. Shirer, *Berlin Diary*. New York: Knopf, 1941, p. 43.
57. Quoted in Shirer, *The Rise and Fall of the Third Reich*, p. 293.
58. Quoted in Shirer, *The Rise and Fall of the Third Reich*, p. 293.
59. Quoted in Fischer, *Nazi Germany*, p. 407.
60. Quoted in Fischer, *Nazi Germany*, p. 412.
61. Quoted in Jarman, *The Rise and Fall of Nazi Germany*, p. 226.

62. Quoted in Shirer, *The Rise and Fall of the Third Reich*, p. 326.

63. Quoted in Fischer, *Nazi Germany*, p. 416.

64. Quoted in Fischer, *Nazi Germany*, p. 417.

65. Quoted in Shirer, *The Rise and Fall of the Third Reich*, p. 329.

66. Quoted in Jarman, *The Rise and Fall of Nazi Germany*, p. 230.

67. Quoted in Fischer, *Nazi Germany*, p. 419.

68. Quoted in Jarman, *The Rise and Fall of Nazi Germany*, p. 232.

69. Quoted in Shirer, *The Rise and Fall of the Third Reich*, p. 347.

Chapter Six: The Road to War: Czechoslovakia and Poland

70. Quoted in Bullock, *Hitler*, p. 443.

71. Quoted in Shirer, *The Rise and Fall of the Third Reich*, p. 361.

72. Quoted in Jarman, *The Rise and Fall of Nazi Germany*, p. 235.

73. Quoted in Shirer, *The Rise and Fall of the Third Reich*, p. 364.

74. Quoted in Shirer, *The Rise and Fall of the Third Reich*, p. 381.

75. Quoted in Bullock, *Hitler*, p. 453.

76. Quoted in Shirer, *The Rise and Fall of the Third Reich*, p. 384.

77. Quoted in Jarman, *The Rise and Fall of Nazi Germany*, p. 455.

78. Quoted in Shirer, *The Rise and Fall of the Third Reich*, p. 387.

79. Quoted in Bullock, *Hitler*, p. 457.

80. Quoted in Shirer, *The Rise and Fall of the Third Reich*, p. 417.

81. Quoted in Shirer, *The Rise and Fall of the Third Reich*, p. 412.

82. Quoted in Shirer, *The Rise and Fall of the Third Reich*, p. 451.

83. Quoted in Shirer, *The Rise and Fall of the Third Reich*, p. 456.

84. Quoted in Shirer, *The Rise and Fall of the Third Reich*, p. 457.

85. Quoted in Shirer, *The Rise and Fall of the Third Reich*, p. 461.

86. Quoted in Fischer, *Nazi Germany*, p. 435.

87. Quoted in Shirer, *The Rise and Fall of the Third Reich*, p. 477.

88. Quoted in Shirer, *The Rise and Fall of the Third Reich*, p. 481.

89. Quoted in Shirer, *The Rise and Fall of the Third Reich*, p. 491.

90. Quoted in Shirer, *The Rise and Fall of the Third Reich*, p. 495.

91. Quoted in Shirer, *The Rise and Fall of the Third Reich*, p. 505.

92. Quoted in Shirer, *The Rise and Fall of the Third Reich*, p. 484.

93. Quoted in Shirer, *The Rise and Fall of the Third Reich*, p. 509.

94. Quoted in Shirer, *The Rise and Fall of the Third Reich*, p. 512.

95. Quoted in Shirer, *The Rise and Fall of the Third Reich*, p. 526.

96. Quoted in Shirer, *The Rise and Fall of the Third Reich*, p. 568.

Chapter Seven: The Third Reich at War

97. Shirer, *Berlin Diary*, p. 200.

98. Shirer, *Berlin Diary*, p. 201.

99. Quoted in Bullock, *Hitler*, p. 550.

100. Quoted in Shirer, *The Rise and Fall of the Third Reich*, p. 517.

101. Shirer, *Berlin Diary*, p. 486.

102. Quoted in Fischer, *Nazi Germany*, p. 535.

103. Quoted in Jarman, *The Rise and Fall of Nazi Germany*, p. 329.

104. Quoted in Bullock, *Hitler*, p. 770.

105. Quoted in Fischer, *Nazi Germany*, p. 443.

106. Quoted in Bullock, *Hitler*, p. 766.

107. Quoted in Bullock, *Hitler*, p. 795.

Epilogue: The Tragedy of "What If?"

108. Quoted in Shirer, *The Rise and Fall of the Third Reich*, p. 239.

109. Shirer, *The Rise and Fall of the Third Reich*, p. 232.

110. Quoted in Fischer, *Nazi Germany*, p. 364.

⭐ Chronology of Events ⭐

1889

April 20: Adolf Hitler born in Braunau am Inn, Austria.

1907

October: Hitler fails entrance examination for Vienna Academy of Art.

1909–1913

Hitler lives as vagrant in Vienna.

1914

August: World War I breaks out; Hitler enlists in German army.

1918

November 11: Germany signs armistice ending World War I.

1919

January 2: German Workers Party founded in Munich by Karl Harrer and Anton Drexler.

February: New German constitution drafted in Weimar.

September 16: Hitler becomes member of German Workers Party.

1920

February 24: Hitler outlines German Workers Party platform in speech in Munich.

March: German Workers Party changes name to National Socialist German Workers Party, soon becomes known as Nazi Party.

1921

Summer: Hitler puts down inner-party dissent, becomes absolute leader of Nazis, establishes *Sturmabteilung* (SA).

1923

March: Hitler establishes *Stabswache*, forerunner of SS.

November 8–9: Nazis' Beer-Hall Putsch in Munich fails.

November 11: Hitler arrested and imprisoned.

1924

February 24: Hitler and other Nazi leaders placed on trial for high treason.

April 1: Hitler sentenced to five years in prison, begins to write *Mein Kampf.*

May 4: First Nazis elected to German Reichstag.

December 20: Hitler released from prison on parole.

1925

February 24: Nazi Party, banned after Beer-Hall Putsch, re-formed in Munich.

April: Ernst Röhm leaves Germany after dispute with Hitler.

April 26: Former Field Marshal Paul von Hindenburg elected president of Germany.

1927

August 19: First Nazi Party rally in Nuremberg.

July 14: First volume of *Mein Kampf* published.

1928

May 20: Nazis receive 2.6 percent of vote in Reichstag elections.

1929

January 6: Heinrich Himmler made head of SS.

October 29: Stock market crashes in United States setting off worldwide economic depression.

1930

March: Hermann Müller replaced as chancellor of Germany by Heinrich Brüning.

September 2: Hitler assumes supreme leadership of SA.

September 14: Nazis gain 18 percent of vote in Reichstag elections.

1931

October 10: Hitler's first meeting with Hindenburg.

1932

February 25: Hitler officially made a German citizen.

March 13: Hitler finishes strong second to Hindenburg in presidential election.

April 10: Hindenburg defeats Hitler in runoff election for presidency.

April 13: Chancellor Brüning bans SA and SS.

May 30: Brüning resigns as chancellor, replaced by Franz von Papen.

June 16: Papen lifts ban on SA and SS.

July 31: Nazis become largest party in Reichstag.

August 13: Hitler refuses offer of a cabinet post after Hindenburg denies his demand to be named chancellor.

November 17: Papen agrees to resign as chancellor.

December 2: Kurt von Schleicher appointed chancellor.

1933

January 4: First secret meeting between Hitler and Papen.

January 28: Schleicher resigns as chancellor.

January 30: Hitler appointed chancellor.

February 27: Fire destroys Reichstag building.

February 28: Hitler given emergency powers to suspend civil liberties.

March 13: Joseph Goebbels made minister for public enlightenment and propaganda.

March 23: Reichstag passes Enabling Act giving Hitler absolute power.

April 1: National boycott of Jewish businesses.

April 7: First of anti-Jewish laws passed by Reichstag.

April 26: Geheime Staatspolizei (Gestapo) established.

May 10: Burning throughout Germany of books by Jewish and liberal authors.

May 17: Hitler says in speech that Germany has no plans to rearm.

July 14: Nazis proclaimed only political party in Germany.

October 14: Germany withdraws from international disarmament conference and League of Nations.

1934

January 26: Hitler announced nonaggression treaty with Poland.

March: Sicherheitsdienst (SD) formed.

June 30: Hitler's opponents killed in Blood Purge.

July 20: SS made independent of SA.

July 25: Nazi takeover of Austria fails.

August 2: President Hindenburg dies; Hitler combines offices of president and chancellor, becoming Führer of Germany; military officers made to pledge personal loyalty to Hitler.

1935

January 13: Citizens of Saar Valley vote overwhelmingly to be made part of Germany.

March 16: Hitler announces military draft, formation of *Luftwaffe.*

June 18: Germany and Great Britain sign naval treaty.

September 15: Nuremberg Laws strip Jews of rights as citizens.

October 3: Mussolini's Italy invades Ethiopia.

1936

March 7: German troops reoccupy the Rhineland.

Summer: Olympic Games held in Berlin; anti-Jewish activity halted.

October 21: Germany and Italy sign treaty of cooperation.

1937

January 30: Hitler declares Treaty of Versailles void.

1938

March: Germany annexes Austria.

April: Germans in Czechoslovakian Sudetenland demand freedom.

September 29–30: Britain and France agree to give Germany part of Czechoslovakia in Munich Agreement.

November 9–10: SS mobs destroy Jewish shops and synagogues in *Kristallnacht* riots.

1939

March 31: British government announces unconditional support of Poland.

May 22: Italy and Germany sign "Pact of Steel" military alliance.

May 23: Hitler informs military leaders that war with Poland is inevitable.

August 23: Germany and Soviet Union sign nonaggression pact in Moscow.

September 1: Germany invades Poland.

September 3: France and Britain declare war on Germany; World War II begins.

1940

May 10: Germany attacks France, Belgium, the Netherlands, and Luxembourg.

June 21: France signs surrender to Germany at Compiègne.

August 13: Battle of Britain begins as German bombers strike British airfields.

1941

June 22: Germany invades Soviet Union.

September 23: Poison gases tested at Auschwitz concentration camp in Poland.

December 4: Soviet army launches counterattack near Moscow.

December 7: Japan attacks U.S. naval base at Pearl Harbor.

December 11: Germany declares war on United States.

December 16: Hitler assumes personal command of all German armed forces.

1942

June 23: Full-scale gassings begin at Auschwitz.

November 5: German troops in North Africa defeated by British in Battle of El Alamein.

November 19: Soviets launch counteroffensive against Germans at Stalingrad.

1943

February 2: Soviets recapture Stalingrad.

September 3: Allied troops land in Italy.

1944

June 6: Allied troops land on beaches of Normandy in France.

July 20: Hitler injured in assassination attempt by Claus von Stauffenberg.

1945

January 14: East Prussia invaded by Soviet troops.

March 7: American troops cross the Rhine River into Germany.

April 23: Soviet troops reach outskirts of Berlin.

April 30: Hitler commits suicide in bunker underneath Berlin.

May 2: Fall of Berlin to Soviets.

May 7: Admiral Karl Dönitz signs unconditional surrender of Germany.

November 20: Top Nazis go on trial in Nuremberg.

1946

October 15: Göring commits suicide in prison.

October 16: Nine top Nazis hanged in Nuremberg prison.

★ For Further Reading ★

David A. Adler, *Child of the Warsaw Ghetto.* New York: Holiday House, 1995. Fictional account of life in the Warsaw ghetto, the uprising against the Nazis, and imprisonment in Auschwitz told through the eyes of a Jewish boy. Excellent illustrations by Karen Ritz. For younger readers.

Susan D. Bachrach, *Tell Them We Remember.* Boston: Little, Brown, 1994. Published for the U.S. Holocaust Memorial Museum. The entire story of the Holocaust, from the rise of the Nazis to the liberation of the concentration camps during World War II, told in short chapters. Liberally illustrated. Photographs of actual Holocaust victims and survivors are most touching.

Bruce Bliven Jr., *From Casablanca to Berlin.* New York: Random House, 1965. Simply written, easy-to-read account of World War II in Europe from the Allied landings in North Africa to the surrender of Germany. Relatively few photographs.

Edward F. Dolan, *Portrait in Tyranny.* New York: Dodd, Mead, 1981. Moderately difficult biography of the leader Adolf Hitler. Text is well organized, but all the photographs are clustered in a central section.

Sarel Eimerl, *Hitler over Europe: The Road to World War II.* Boston: Little, Brown, 1972. Comprehensive account of the years from 1929 to 1939 covering the Nazis' seizure of power and the events leading to World War II.

Brendan John Elliott, *Hitler and Germany.* New York: McGraw-Hill, 1968. Excellent account of Hitler's rise and fall. Especially valuable in that it gives the background factors in Germany that made Nazism possible.

Albert Marrin, *Hitler.* New York: Viking Kestrel, 1987. Superior biography of Hitler for the more advanced reader complete with primary-source quotations and a good variety of photographs.

Joshua Rubenstein, *Adolf Hitler.* New York: Franklin Watts, 1984. Volume in the Impact Biography series. Biographical account of the rise and fall of the Nazi leader. Good, moderately difficult text but short on photographs.

G. C. Skipper, *Death of Hitler.* Chicago: Children's Press, 1980. Volume in the World at War series. Insertions of fictional conversation mar this otherwise good account of Hitler's final days. Outstanding collection of photographs.

———, *Göring and the Luftwaffe*. Chicago: Children's Press, 1980. Volume in the World at War series. Excellent biography of Hermann Göring and description of the German air force and its attacks on Poland and Great Britain.

R. Conrad Stein, *Hitler Youth*. Chicago: Children's Press, 1985. Volume in the World at War series. Simply written account of how the Nazis tried to take control of the minds of children in Germany. Plenty of photographs.

Richard Tames, *Nazi Germany*. London: Batsford Academic and Educational, 1985. Volume in the Living Through History series. Short account of the Nazis' rise to power and minibiographies of the leading Nazis and some of those who opposed them.

Harold Cecil Vaughn, *The Versailles Treaty*. New York: Franklin Watts, 1975. Designed for the serious, more advanced student, but a very thorough account of the treaty that ended World War I and its consequences, both immediate and long-term.

★ Works Consulted ★

Yehuda Bauer, *A History of the Holocaust.* New York: Franklin Watts, 1982. One of the world's foremost authorities describes both the Holocaust and the events leading to it. Charts and maps help the reader get an accurate picture.

Karl Dietrich Bracher, *The German Dictatorship.* Translated by Jean Steinberg. New York: Praeger, 1971. Very scholarly in tone and thus not as readable as some other accounts, but a very comprehensive examination of the Third Reich.

Alan Bullock, *Hitler: A Study in Tyranny.* New York: Harper & Row, 1962. A revised edition of the original work published in 1951, this remains probably the best of all the Hitler biographies.

Joachim C. Fest, *The Face of the Third Reich.* New York: Pantheon, 1970. Deep and often disturbing examination of the inner motives that drove some of the leading figures of the Nazi Party.

Klaus P. Fischer, *Nazi Germany: A New History.* New York: Continuum, 1995. An excellent and complete overview of the roots of the Nazi Party, its rise to power, and its destruction.

Otto Friedrich, *Before the Deluge: A Portrait of Berlin in the 1920's.* New York: Harper & Row, 1972. A good look at life in Germany during the early days of the Weimar Republic when the Nazis were gaining power.

Daniel Jonah Goldhagen, *Hitler's Willing Executioners.* New York: Knopf, 1996. Excellent study of how ordinary Germans, not just fanatical Nazis, were willing participants in the Holocaust.

Rudolf Höss, Pery Broad, and Johann Paul Kremer, *KL Auschwitz Seen by the SS.* Edited by Jadwiga Bezwinska and Danuta Czech. Translated by Constantine Fitzgibbon, Krystyna Michalik, and Zbigniew Bezwinski. New York: Howard Fertig, 1984. Excerpts from the writings of three veteran SS officers give valuable insight into the frame of mind of those who worked in the death camps.

T. L. Jarman, *The Rise and Fall of Nazi Germany.* New York: New York University Press, 1956. Does not have the massive detail of some other summaries but still a good, highly readable history.

August Kubizek, *The Young Hitler I Knew.* Westport, CT: Greenwood Press, 1976. By far the best account of Adolf Hitler's youth, written by his best and perhaps only boyhood friend.

Walter Laquer, *Weimar: A Cultural History 1918–1933*. New York: Putnam's, 1974. Very detailed examination of cultural and intellectual developments in the Weimar Republic, many of which directly influenced the growth of the Nazis.

Jeremy Noakes and Geoffrey Pridham, *Foreign Policy, War, and Racial Extermination*. Exeter, England: University of Exeter Press, 1988. Volume 3 of the series *Nazism, 1919–1945, a Documentary Reader*. The story of the Holocaust is told in quotations from speeches, letters, and other documents by the participants, both perpetrators and victims.

Dietrich Orlow, *The History of the Nazi Party: 1919–1933*. Pittsburgh, PA: University of Pittsburgh Press, 1969. Scholarly, often dry account of the Nazi rise to power. Frequent statistical tables are interesting but tend to bog down narrative.

William L. Shirer, *Berlin Diary*. New York: Knopf, 1941. Day-by-day account of how Hitler and the Nazis plunged the world into war, from the diary of an American journalist.

———, *The Rise and Fall of the Third Reich*. New York: Simon & Schuster, 1959. Written by an award-winning journalist, this is one of the most comprehensive and readable of the histories of Nazi Germany.

Louis L. Snyder, *The Encyclopedia of the Third Reich*. New York: Paragon House, 1989. An indispensable tool for anyone studying Nazi Germany. All the major people, places, and events are described in short articles in alphabetical order.

John Weiss, *Ideology of Death: Why the Holocaust Happened in Germany*. Chicago: Ivan R. Dee, 1996. Explores the course of history in Germany and Austria and the character of their people in order to explain the Holocaust.

★ Index ★

★ Picture Credits ★

Cover photo: Digital Stock
Archive Photos, 7 (bottom)
Archive Photos/Leo Baeck Institute, 47
Archive Photos/Popperfoto, 57
Archives of the Simon Wiesenthal Center, 7 (top), 8, 48
Corbis-Bettmann, 70
Corbis/Hulton-Deutsch Collection, 20 (bottom)
Corbis/Underwood & Underwood, 71
Courtesy of USHMM Photo Archives, 51
Digital Stock, 5
Dokumentationsarchiv des Osterreichischen Widerstandes, courtesy of USHMM Photo Archives, 54
FPG International, 23 (bottom), 55 (bottom), 73, 85, 90
Imperial War Museum/Archive Photos, 40, 41, 79 (top), 87
Joseph Paris Picture Archives, 17, 22, 25, 29, 32, 36, 37, 39, 62, 92, 94
Library of Congress, 11 (both), 13, 24, 26, 43 (bottom), 76, 77
Main Commission for the Investigation of Nazi War Crimes, courtesy of USHMM Photo Archives, 43 (top), 53
National Archives, 9 (both), 18, 20 (top), 23 (top), 27, 33 (both), 35, 55 (top), 59, 63, 64, 67 (both), 69, 74, 79 (bottom)
National Archives, courtesy of USHMM Photo Archives, 50, 93
Smithsonian Institute, 83

☆ About the Author ☆

William W. Lace is a native of Fort Worth, Texas. He holds a bachelor's degree from Texas Christian University, a master's from East Texas State University, and a doctorate from the University of North Texas. After working for newspapers in Baytown, Texas, and Fort Worth, he joined the University of Texas at Arlington as sports information director and later became the director of the news service. He is now executive assistant to the chancellor for the Tarrant County College District in Fort Worth. He and his wife, Laura, live in Arlington and have two children. Lace has written numerous other works for Lucent Books, one of which—*The Death Camps* in the Holocaust Library series—was selected by the New York Public Library for its 1999 Recommended Teenage Reading List.